Greetings!

Greetings!

Culture and Speaking Skills for Intermediate Students of English

Meredith Westfall

Ann Arbor THE UNIVERSITY OF MICHIGAN PRESS

ISBN 0-472-08507-7
Published in the United States of America by
The University of Michigan Press
Manufactured in the United States of America

2001 2000 4 3 2

To Andreas, a Tokyo treasure

Acknowledgments

I would like to thank my family and friends, who have all been very supportive and understanding through the whole process of writing this book. Joshua Fujiwara, the computer doctor, helped me with his incredible knowledge of computers. Maybelle O. Ruiz contributed her knowledge about the Philippines. Weldon C. Doran did a great job putting his art skills to use. DaNice Marshall, a terrific writer, has become a welcome new friend. I must acknowledge all of my students at Inner Mongolia University (in Hohhot, China), the Foreign Language International Institute (in Numazu, Japan), CELOP (at Boston University), Brookline Adult Community Education Program, and the English Language Center (in Boston). I searched high and low for the author of the poem entitled "Rainbows" but failed, so if you are out there I want to thank you for your terrific verse I used in unit eleven. Without all of you and your questions, I never would have had the ideas and material to create this textbook. Kelly Sippell and the reviewers at the University of Michigan did their jobs by answering all of my questions and giving clear advice on what to do next. And most importantly, I would like to express my deep gratitude to Steven Molinsky for his ideas, encouragement, and inspiration.

Grateful acknowledgment is given for use of the following copyrighted material:

DaNice Marshall for the poem "Aged."

Brøderbund Software, Inc., graphics courtesy of The Print Shop Deluxe®;

Introduction

Greetings! is a twelve-unit conversation textbook for adults and young adults at the intermediate level. *Greetings!* revolves around special occasions in the United States and the greeting cards people send to acknowledge and/or celebrate them. This textbook is to be used along with supplemental material in order to give students guided practice in speaking activities.

Each unit presents students with one topic and then engages them with related activities such as writing captions for greeting cards, finding solutions to various problems, and answering discussion questions about each topic. In every unit, students are given a lot of opportunities to share personal information and opinions. In addition, each unit gives students a chance to practice functional language including, but not limited to, inviting, sympathizing, apologizing, and expressing gratitude.

Each unit in *Greetings!* provides material for approximately five one-hour classes, depending on how much time the teacher devotes to each activity. The units are flexible, so it is not imperative that the teacher follow any particular sequence. It should be noted, however, that the units are organized to correspond to the natural milestones one goes through in life.

Many of the activities in *Greetings!* try to pull in the knowledge ESL students bring with them into the classroom. When talking about customs, students should be encouraged to talk about their own experiences. Because the themes in *Greetings!* are universal, all students have many chances to join in the classroom discussions. This assumes that students are more comfortable when talking about topics with which they are familiar. The end result is a classroom where students are motivated and talkative.

To the Teacher

Throughout the book, some idioms are printed in bold type to let you and the student know that they are listed in the glossary at the end of the book. Depending on the level of your students, you may want to spend extra time on confusing idioms or difficult vocabulary before starting on a lesson. You could preview the lesson with your students to see what they know, what they don't know, and what they want to learn in the upcoming unit.

Within each unit, there are many possibilities for expansion activities. Below are just a few ideas of how to go beyond the unit. Students could . . .

- write about their own personal experience at a particular event or celebration.
- take a field trip to a museum or local art gallery and find paintings that could be used as images for greeting cards.
- have an "art day" where they bring in materials to make their own greeting cards.
- learn about the rhythm used in poetry. Students could use nursery rhymes and incorporate them into their own poems related to the special occasion they are learning about at a particular time.
- visit the library and do more in-depth research on one aspect of a particular event being discussed.

By no means should you, as a teacher, feel limited to follow the lesson as it stands. You might want to change the directions, supplement a particular unit with your own material, or add more grammar or idiom practice when necessary.

To the Student

You are about to explore many aspects of American culture. While you are doing this, you will probably learn more about your own culture as well. To be a successful student, you have to take risks. Don't worry about making mistakes because sometimes communication is more important than a grammatically correct sentence.

You will see that some words and phrases are printed in bold type throughout the book. That is because they are listed in the glossary with a definition. In English, there are many idioms that can be confusing to English language learners, so don't be afraid to ask if you don't understand. When you are reading and find a word or phrase you do not know, you can always guess its meaning and continue on. Sometimes it is not necessary to understand every word of what you are reading. You also might want to have a good dictionary with you.

Contents

Unit 1
Keep in Touch

How Do We Communicate?

In a group, talk about some ways people communicate with each other. Be sure to list them below. Write at least one advantage and one disadvantage for each method.

Method	Advantage	Disadvantage
inexpensive	letters	slow

What method do you use most often? Least often? Why?

I'm Thinking of . . .

Pair up with another student; one of you is Student A and the other is Student B. Student A will choose one of the objects pictured above. Student A will not tell Student B what it is. Student B will ask Student A questions that can be answered with either a yes or a no to try to determine which object Student A selected.

"Do you use this every day?" "Yes, I do."
"Do you need electricity to use this?" "No, I don't."
"Is it expensive?" "No, it isn't."
"Is it heavy?" "No, it isn't."
"Is it a pencil?" "Yes, it is."

What Are Greeting Cards?

Greeting cards are sold **all over** America. Drugstores (also called pharmacies) and supermarkets are two places that sell them. Greeting cards have been available in America since the 1800s, but most of these cards were for holidays such as Christmas and Valentine's Day. Greeting cards one gives for personal occasions, such as a birthday or graduation, became popular much later—in the 1950s or so.

Greeting cards **fall into** two categories, cards for special occasions (for example, birthdays) and cards for holidays. The ones for special occasions are available throughout the year, but holiday cards are seasonal, or available only weeks before the holiday. The "everyday" special occasion cards are becoming more and more popular. There are even some cards that acknowledge a pet's birthday! If one spends time looking at the various occasions in a particular culture for which cards exist, he or she will learn a lot about that culture.

Greeting cards can convey many different messages and tones. Some cards are very **sentimental,** while others are humorous. Many of the more serious cards are religious. For most cards, it is easy to see who the intended audience is. For example, a birthday card with teddy bears on it is probably for a child, while one with hearts on it is for that special person you love.

Picking out the right card can be difficult because there are so many choices. You must also consider the relationship between you, the sender, and the receiver of the card. The chances are very good that you will find the perfect card for each occasion.

Holidays

1. Valentine's Day
2.
3.
4.
5.
6.
7.
8.
9.
10.

Special Occasions

1. Birthday
2.
3.
4.
5.
6.
7.
8.
9.
10.

Talking about Greeting Cards

Work in groups and answer the questions. Be prepared to tell the whole class what you talked about.

Questions:

1. Name some additional places where you can buy greeting cards.
   drugstores
   supermarkets
   ____
   ____
   ____
   ____
   ____
2. Do you buy greeting cards? If so, how often do you buy them, and what kinds do you buy? ____________________
3. Do you enjoy sending greeting cards? Why or why not? ____________________
   ____
4. Do you enjoy receiving cards? Why or why not? ____________________
   ____
5. Are greeting cards sold in your country? If so, for what occasions? ________
   ____
6. Is it popular in your country to send or give greeting cards? ____________
   ____
7. Do you save old greeting cards? If so, from whom? ____________________
   ____
8. When was the last time you sent a greeting card? What was the occasion? ___
   ____
9. How often do you write letters? ____________________
10. How often do you visit friends? Can you just drop in, or do you have to call first?____________________
11. Do you think e-mail will replace handwritten letters? Why or why not? ____
    ____
12. Which do you prefer, talking face-to-face or talking on the phone? Why? ___
    ____

13. Do you like cellular phones? Why or why not? ______________________
____

14. Imagine you could never use the phone again. How would your life be different? ____

If I could never use the phone again, I would have to ______________________ .
My life would be very different because ______________________ .
If I never used the phone again, I ______________________ .
I like using the phone because ______________________ .
I don't always enjoy using the phone because ______________________ .

Keeping in Touch

Read the situations below. Consider all of the possible answers and then choose the best answer. Form groups, then as a group come up with one more possible answer for each scenario.

1. You want to let your friends know that you got a job promotion. What would you do?
   a. I would call them.
   b. I would send them a letter.
   c. I would send them e-mail.
   d. ____
2. It's your friend's birthday. Your friend lives far away in another country. What would you do?
   a. I would send a birthday card.
   b. I would call and talk for an hour.
   c. I would forget about it. My friend lives too far away.
   d. ____
3. Someone you know has died. How would you like to find out about it?
   a. I would like to hear about it by phone.
   b. I would like to get a letter.
   c. I would like to read about it in the newspaper.
   d. ____

4. You want to break up with your boy/girlfriend. How would you do it?
   a. I would do it over a nice dinner at a restaurant.
   b. I would send a card saying I want to end the relationship.
   c. I would do it over the phone.
   d. ______________________________

You might want to use the conversation helpers below while you are discussing the situations above.

If I were in that situation, I would ______________________________
____

This never happened to me, but if it did, I would ______________________________
____

This actually happened to me. I ______________________________
____

Secret Admirers

In this exercise, you will be writing a card to one of your classmates, but you will not be signing your name. You will be **anonymous.**

1. Write your name on a piece of paper.
2. The teacher will collect all of the pieces of paper in a hat or box.
3. When it's your turn, pick a piece of paper out of the hat or box. The name on the paper is the person you will be writing to. DON'T SHOW ANYONE THE NAME YOU PICK. IT'S A SECRET **FOR NOW.**
4. For homework, make or buy a card. Then write a short note to your secret friend. If you don't know what to write about, you might think about introducing yourself and then talking about your hobbies or other things that interest you.
5. When you are finished writing, DON'T SIGN YOUR NAME. Instead, sign it "From a Secret Admirer." And don't forget to address the envelope.
6. Bring the card to the next class.
7. Give the card to the teacher, who will then deliver them.
8. Spend time walking around asking your classmates questions. Try to find out who your secret admirer is. When asking questions, don't ask: "Did you write

this card?" Instead, ask questions about what was written in the letter you received. Some possible examples:

"Do you like cats?" or "Are you from Argentina?" or "How many brothers do you have?"

Look at an example of a short note.

```
Dear Maria,
You don't know who I am. I like cats, have four
brothers, and play tennis once a week.
                    From,
                    A Secret Admirer
```

Here are some ideas of what to write.

I have ______________________________.

I know how to ______________________________.

When I was a child, I ______________________________.

I want to ______________________________.

Discussing a Card

Look around your house and find a card that you have received. If you don't have one, borrow one from someone you know. If that isn't possible, go to a card shop and find a card that you would like to discuss. You don't have to buy the card. You can sketch or write about the image and write down the caption in the space on page 8.

The Image

An image is the picture on the card.

The Caption

The caption is the printed message inside the card.

1. Draw the image of the card you chose to discuss in the box under "The Image." If you don't want to draw the image, then write about it instead.
2. Write the caption of the card you chose to discuss in the box under "The Caption." ______
3. Did someone send this card to you? If so, who? ______
4. What was the occasion? ______
5. Do you like this card? Why or why not? ______
6. Do you keep in touch with this person? If so, how often? ______
7. How long ago did you receive this card? ______
8. Do you ever send cards to this person? Under what circumstances? ______
   ______
9. Do you keep letters or do you throw them out? ______
10. How do you decide which letters and cards to keep and which ones to throw out? ______
11. Using the card you chose, how would you rewrite the caption in your own words? ______

Unit 2
It's a Boy. It's a Girl.

Heard there's a new little bundle in your family. What terrific news.

Make a list of words you think of when you think of babies.

______________	______________	______________	______________
______________	______________	______________	______________
______________	______________	______________	______________
______________	______________	______________	______________

Announcing a New Member of the Family

The birth of a baby is wonderful news for all involved, especially the parents. It is quite common for American parents to send a birth announcement letting everyone know the big news. Most traditional birth announcements include the full name of the baby, the parents' names, and the parents' address. In addition, they will provide information about the weight of the baby given in pounds and ounces and the length of the baby given in inches. If the card is printed, the parents will usually personalize it with a short note.

However, not all birth announcements are traditional. One family sent the baby's footprints and included a photograph. Another family sent a cassette tape recording of the baby crying. The parents sent a letter with the cassette. This is what it said.

The loud voice you just heard came from a future baseball great. His name is Tyler.

Answer the questions on your own. Then discuss them in small groups.

1.	People in my country send birth announcements.	true	false
2.	I like traditional birth announcements the best.	true	false
3.	Sending creative birth announcements is **a waste of time.**	true	false
4.	I have never received a birth announcement.	true	false

If you circled "false" for any of your answers, rewrite the sentence to make it true.

____

____

____

In your group, think of two more creative ways Tyler's parents could have announced the birth of their son.

1. They could have ______________________________
2. They could have ______________________________

After you have made your list, choose one of the two ideas and rewrite Tyler's birth announcement on a separate piece of paper.

Two Poems about You

What kind of words are used to describe people? Look at the lists below. Add at least five new words to each list.

Physical traits	Personality	Action words	Occupations
tall	generous	paints	lawyer
strong	friendly	plays tennis	student
young	funny	reads	policeman
pretty	intelligent	watches TV	cashier
________	________	________	________
________	________	________	________
________	________	________	________
________	________	________	________
________	________	________	________

You are going to write a poem using the cinquain format. "Cinquain" means the poem will have five lines. Look at the model.

Title: (the name of the person the poem is about)

One noun: (occupation)
Two adjectives: (personality and/or appearance)
Three verbs: (action words that describe the person's hobbies. Use present tense.)
Any phrase: (a bunch of words)
One word: (a word that sums up the person)

Example:
Tina
Artist
Creative, active
Paints, runs, sings
Full of energy
Alive

Using the poem about Tina as a model, write two poems about yourself.

1. Write a poem about yourself when you were a child.
2. Write a poem that describes yourself now.

as a child:

____
____
____
____
____

now:

____
____
____
____
____

Extra practice:
After you finish writing your two poems, write another one about someone you know. Read the poem aloud and have your classmates guess who your poem is about.

____
____
____
____
____

The Interview

Work with a partner and take turns interviewing each other. When you are done, report one interesting fact you learned about your partner to the class.

1. In what month were you born? ______
2. What's your **sign**? ______
3. Do you think boys or girls have it easier? ______
4. Would you like to have an identical twin? Why or why not? ______
5. If you had to pick one age to be and stay there for the rest of your life, what age would you pick? Why? ______
6. Based on stories you've heard about yourself, what were you like as a baby? ______
7. On what day were you born? ______
8. What is your earliest childhood memory? How old were you? ______
9. How many brothers and sisters do you have? ______
10. Would you like to know the sex of your child before becoming a parent? Why or why not? ______
11. Do you think you were **spoiled** as a child? ______
12. List five ways you can tell that a child is spoiled.

13. Working with a partner or in a small group, look at the chart below. Write some advantages and disadvantages for each situation.

Situation	Advantage	Disadvantage
Having lots of brothers and sisters	never lonely	noisy
Having only one brother or sister		
Being the only child		
Being the oldest child		
Being the youngest child		
Being the middle child		

When I Was a Child . . .

Think about and then list some places **associated** with children.

toy store __________ __________ __________

What are some activities associated with children?

fingerpainting __________ __________ __________

What are some foods associated with children?

pudding __________ __________ __________

Sentence practice:

Using the words in the box, write sentences about yourself when you were a child.

always,	usually,	often,	sometimes,	rarely,	seldom,	hardly ever,	never
100%		80%	50%	20%		5%	0%

Example:
When I was a child, I always went to the beach and drew pictures in the sand.
When I was a child, I never ate liver because I hated it.

1. When I was a child, I always ______________________________ .
2. When I was a child, I usually ______________________________ .
3. When I was a child, I often ______________________________ .
4. When I was a child, I sometimes ______________________________ .
5. When I was a child, I rarely ______________________________ .
6. When I was a child, I seldom ______________________________ .
7. When I was a child, I hardly ever ______________________________ .
8. When I was a child, I never ______________________________ .
9. When I was a child, I ______________________________ .
10. When I was a child, I ______________________________ .

When you are finished, discuss what you wrote with a partner. Then complete the sentences below.

Both my partner and I ______________________________ .
I was surprised to learn that my partner ______________________________ .
I never knew that my partner ______________________________ .
My partner was very lucky/unlucky because ______________________________ .

If I Were in That Situation . . .

Look at the situations below. Read all of the possible answers and choose the best one. Then work in a group and create one more answer for each scenario.

1. You and a friend are at a very fancy restaurant eating dinner when a family with three children sits at the next table. One of the children starts to cry, and the parents are unable to get the child to stop. What would you do?
   a. I would ask the server if we could change our table.
   b. I would ignore it. I was a child a long time ago.
   c. I would eat very quickly and leave.
   d. ______________________________

2. Your friends are proud new parents of a little baby boy. You are surprised to see that the baby is not very cute. What do you tell the parents when they ask you what you think about little Richard?
   a. I would tell them that their baby is one of the cutest babies I have ever seen.
   b. I would tell them that the baby's clothes are very pretty.
   c. I would say very little and then change the subject.
   d. ______________________________
3. Your friends are planning to take their one-year-old baby on a two-month trip to Europe. What would you say to them?
   a. "Good luck."
   b. "I wouldn't if I were you."
   c. "Have a good trip. Don't forget to send me a postcard."
   d. "______________________________."
4. You are going to be a parent. The doctor knows if it is going to be a boy or a girl. What do you say to the doctor?
   a. "Please tell me."
   b. "Please don't tell me. I want it to be a surprise."
   c. "Let me think about it. Ask me in a month if I want to know."
   d. "______________________________."

In a group: Use the possible scenarios above as a model. On another sheet of paper, write your own situation and give three possible solutions. When you are finished, exchange your paper with one from a different group. Discuss the new situation with your group and agree on one answer. If you don't like the answers you were given, write a new one. Act out your situation (but not your answer) in front of your classmates and let them think of a solution. See if they can match the solution your group chose. After they have chosen a solution continue acting out the end of your situation.

I Was Born!

Create your own (or your friend's, brother's, sister's, spouse's, child's) birth announcement.

You might want to include

the full name of the baby
the birth date
the names and address of the parents
the hour of the birth
the name of the hospital
the birth weight

Unit 3
Good Luck or Congratulations?

You can do it!

You did it!

1. Look at the two captions above. What is the difference between the two?
   "You can do it" means ______________________________ .
   "You did it" means ______________________________ .
2. Which card would you like to receive? Why?____________________
3. Think of some situations when people use these phrases. Make a list.

"You can do it."	"You did it."
____________________	____________________
____________________	____________________
____________________	____________________
____________________	____________________

What Should I Say?

Choose a partner. In the first dialogue below, one of you will be Tess and one of you will be James. In the second one, one of you will be Bob and one of you will be Sarah. Now, in your roles, practice the dialogue.

Tess and James work together in the same office.

James: Tess, you sure have a big smile on your face.
Tess: I sure do. I passed my road test earlier today.
James: You passed your road test? That's great news. Congratulations.

Bob and Sarah are classmates.

Bob: Sarah, you look a little nervous.
Sarah: I am nervous. I have a job interview tomorrow.
Bob: You have a job interview? Good luck!

Each of the boxes below describes an occasion for which you might say, "Congratulations" or "Good Luck." Write what you would say for each situation. In the box that only says "Congratulations," write an appropriate situation. Do the same for the box that only says "Good Luck." After that, select one situation and act it out with your partner.

You just got a new job. ____________	You are going to ask for a raise. ____________	You have a big exam tomorrow. ____________
You are meeting your fiancé's parents. ____________	You are going to have a baby. ____________	You won the lottery. ____________
You got 550 on the TOEFL. ____________	You ran a marathon. ____________	You have to give a presentation. ____________
? Congratulations!	You bought a new home. ____________	? Good Luck!

Practice the dialogues above with a partner using the information in the boxes. Choose one situation from above to act out with your partner.

Looking for Luck

In a group, ask and answer the questions below.

1. What are some things people use or do to bring good luck? ______________
2. Do you think any of these methods work? Why or why not? ______________
3. When was the last time someone wished you good luck? What was the occasion? ______________
4. When was the last time someone congratulated you? Why? ______________
5. If you had a big job interview coming up, would you tell everyone before it happened or would you wait until after you had it? Why? ______________
6. Fortune-tellers are people who believe they can see into the future. Some can look at tea leaves and tell what is going to happen. What are some other ways fortune-tellers predict what will happen in the future?

   read tea leaves ______________

   ______________ ______________

   ______________ ______________
7. Have you ever been to a fortune-teller? Was your reading accurate? ______________
8. What do you think about **psychics?** ______________
9. Do you read your horoscope in the paper every day? Why or why not? ______________
10. Do you think anyone will be wishing you good luck anytime in the near future? If so, why? ______________

11. What method of fortune-telling is most popular in your country? ________
12. Are you **superstitious?** If so, give some examples. ________________

____

13. Do any numbers have special meaning to you? If so, why? ____________

____

14. What are some superstitions people in your country have? ____________

____

15. Do you believe in ghosts? Why or why not? ____________________

____

16. "You already possess everything necessary to become great."

—Native American proverb

Discuss this proverb. What does it mean? Do you agree or disagree? Why?

Make a wish. Have you ever heard any of these superstitions?

Make a wish every time you eat a green M&M.
Make a wish before you blow out the candles on your birthday cake.
Make a wish on the first star you see at night.
Make a wish when you see your reflection after throwing a coin into a fountain.
Make a wish on a new pair of shoes before you wear them.
Make a wish on the first robin you see in the spring.

What do you do to make your wishes come true?

What Would You Do?

Look at the situations below. Read all of the possible answers and choose the best one. Then work in a group and create one more answer for each scenario.

1. You have a meeting with your boss next week to discuss a possible job promotion. What would you do?
   a. I would **keep quiet.** Talking about it before it happens may bring bad luck.
   b. I would tell everyone. I like it when my friends wish me good luck.
   c. I would only tell my very close friends. If I didn't get the promotion, I would be embarrassed.
   d. ____.

2. What do you do when you see the horoscope page in the newspaper?
   a. I read it. In fact, I read it every day.
   b. I read it if I have time, but I don't believe what it says.
   c. I skip over it. I'm very busy and reading the horoscopes is a huge waste of time.
   d. ______________________________.
3. Your friend has a lucky charm he always wears around his neck. He is also an extremely lucky person. What do you think about this?
   a. He is a very fortunate person.
   b. It is a bit strange, but I still like him.
   c. Perhaps I should get a lucky charm. I've been very unlucky lately.
   d. ______________________________.
4. What do you do when you are at a Chinese restaurant and get the fortune cookie at the end of the meal?
   a. I am very excited, so I am the first to grab a cookie from the plate.
   b. I forget about the cookies. They taste bad, and the fortunes are never accurate.
   c. If asked to, I read my fortune to the rest of the people at the table.
   d. ______________________________.

Fortune Cookies

Have you ever had a fortune cookie at the end of a meal in a Chinese restaurant? Inside each crunchy cookie is a small piece of paper with a fortune written on it. This is an American adaptation of Chinese culture. People in China don't have this custom!

Read the fortunes below. Then write the opposite fortune under each one. Work with a partner.

Now is the time to try something new.	Silence is the key to joy.
______________________	______________________
______________________	______________________
You will be traveling and coming into a lot of adventure.	You are original and creative.
______________________	______________________
______________________	______________________
Keep your credit cards in your wallet.	You will meet someone new.
______________________	______________________
______________________	______________________

1. Which fortune would you like to get? Why? ______________________
2. Which fortune do you think your partner should get? ________________
3. Which fortune best describes your life? __________________________
4. When was the last time you had a fortune cookie? __________________
5. What did the fortune say? __________________________________

Fortune Fun

Everyone writes a fortune on a piece of paper. The teacher will collect them. Pick a new fortune. Walk around the class and try to find the person who wrote yours. Ask questions. Good luck!

Superstition Trivia

Did you know that people in Japan believe a person's blood type influences personality?

Blood type A: diligent, methodical, and nervous
Blood type B: original and fickle
Blood type AB: sociable and sensitive
Blood type O: durable and determined

Questions:

1. Do you know your blood type? If so, don't tell your partner. Have your partner guess what it is based on the information above.
2. Do you think there is any truth to this? ______________________________
3. What does it mean to have a "Type A" personality? ____________________
4. Is there anything like this in your country to determine personality? _______

Other superstitions:

Did you know that the number *4* is unlucky in China? This is because the word *four* sounds like the word for *death* in Chinese.
Did you know that in America many buildings avoid numbering the thirteenth floor? Instead, the numbers go directly from the twelfth floor to the fourteenth floor.
Did you know that people in the Philippines avoid celebrating birthdays before the actual day? They think it could cause an early death.

What superstitions do you know?

In my country people believe_____________________________. This is because
____ .

Share the superstition(s) you wrote down with your classmates.

Sentence practice:
You are an optimist, so you always see the bright side of things!

Write sentences using the words *unfortunately* and *fortunately*. Look at the examples.

Unfortunately, it rained. Fortunately, I had my umbrella with me.
Unfortunately, I lost my homework. Fortunately, the teacher forgot to collect it.

1. Unfortunately, ______________________. Fortunately, ______________ .
2. Unfortunately, ______________________. Fortunately, ______________ .
3. Unfortunately, ______________________. Fortunately, ______________ .
4. Unfortunately, ______________________. Fortunately, ______________ .
5. Unfortunately, ______________________. Fortunately, ______________ .

Work with a partner. You say your "Unfortunately, ____________" sentence and your partner will complete it using a "Fortunately,________________" sentence. After you have practiced, switch roles.

Wish Him Luck or Congratulate Him

Your friend is a struggling actor. He has an audition next Thursday for a major Hollywood film. Send a card wishing him good luck. Write three different "good luck" captions in the boxes next to the first image.

He got the part. Your friend is on his way to Hollywood. Write three different "Congratulations" captions in the boxes next to the second image.

Unit 4
You're Invited

Read the invitation below.

Come to a summer BBQ party.
Where: At John and Beth's house
When: August 25
Why: Beth's birthday
Time: From 4:00pm – ?
What to bring: BYOB. Food will be supplied.
Don't forget your bathing suit.
Be prepared for volleyball.
There will be a boom box, so bring music.
RSVP: 236-6945
Call for directions.

Using the invitation above, which of the following questions can be answered?

1. Who is sending the invitation? ________________
2. What does BBQ mean? ________________
3. Why is there going to be a BBQ party? ________________
4. Where is it going to be? ________________
5. What do you think BYOB means? ________________
6. How many guests have been invited? ________________
7. If a guest wants to go, what should he or she do? ________________
8. What is a boom box? ________________
9. What activities will there be at the BBQ? ________________
10. When does the BBQ begin? ________________

11. What time does it end? ______________________________
12. What kind of food will be served? ______________________________
13. What kind of clothes will the guests be wearing? ______________________________
14. What kind of music will the guests be listening to? ______________________________
15. Where do the hosts of the BBQ party live? ______________________________
16. What types of parties do you like? ______________________________

Welcome

Below you will see several different ways to say "welcome." Try to match the phrase with the language. The answers are at the bottom of the page. Try not to look until you are finished.

1.	__ Huannin	a. Japanese
2.	__ Mabuhay	b. Korean
3.	__ Yoku-Irashai-Mashita	c. East Indian
4.	__ Huan-Young-Hum-Nida	d. Navajo
5.	__ Namaste	e. Italian
6.	__ Buon giorno	f. Swahili
7.	__ Karibu	g. Chinese
8.	__ Yah-Ah-Teeh	h. Filipino

How do you say "welcome" in your language? ______________________________
Spend a few minutes teaching your classmates how to say it.

If you speak any of the languages above, are there any additional ways to say "welcome"?
If so, what are they? ______________________________
What is the difference between welcoming and greeting someone? Ask around and report back to the class.

Answers to the "welcome" quiz
1. g, 2. b, 3. a, 4. b, 5. c, 6. e, 7. f, 8. d

In America, people tend to shake hands when greeting and meeting people. In France, people kiss each cheek of the person they are greeting. Some South Seas Islanders rub noses as a greeting.

How do people in your country greet each other? ______________________

How do you greet a family member? ______________________

How do you greet a good friend? ______________________

How do you greet an acquaintance? ______________________

Do you feel comfortable when people want to greet you with a handshake? ______

Is physical contact important when greeting others in your country? Why or why not? ______________________

On your own: Before the next class, do some people watching. When you are out at the supermarket, in the coffee shop, at the subway station, or anywhere else where people tend to gather, listen to what they say to each other. What did you learn? Report your findings to your classmates.

What Would You Do?

Read the situations below. Review all of the possible answers and then choose the one you think is the best solution. Then work in a group and create one more answer for each scenario.

1. You are invited to a co-worker's house for dinner. This co-worker isn't one of your favorite people. What would you do?
   a. I would go.
   b. I would say that I was busy.
   c. I would say I was going. Then I would cancel at the last minute.
   d. ______________________
2. Your friends are planning to go to an expensive French restaurant for dinner. You want to go, but you don't have enough money for an expensive dinner. What would you do?
   a. I would tell my friends that I couldn't afford such an expensive dinner, so I couldn't go.
   b. I would lie and say I had other plans.
   c. I would borrow money and go.
   d. ______________________

3. You were invited to a wedding but forgot to **RSVP.** The wedding is in one week, and you want to go. What would you do?
   a. I would send a wedding gift but wouldn't go to the wedding.
   b. I would call the bride and groom and explain the situation to them. Hopefully, they would say it was OK.
   c. I would just go to the wedding and hope the RSVP wasn't important.
   d. ______________________________
4. You are at someone's house for dinner. The hostess serves a beautiful dessert that she made. You are on a diet, so you don't want any. You don't want to offend the hostess. What would you say?
   a. "No, thank you." I would stick to my diet.
   b. "Thank you." I would forget about my diet.
   c. "It looks delicious. Could I have a very small piece?" I would worry about my diet the next day.
   d. ______________________________

Discuss these situations with your group.

1. Have you ever been in any situations like these? What did you do?
2. If you were in your country, how would you handle these situations?

Let's Do Something

Work with a partner and practice the role plays provided. Be prepared to act them out in front of the class if your teacher asks you.

Helpful phrases:

<table>
<tr><td>Offering
Would you like to (Verb)________?
How about (Verb) ________ing?
Let's (Verb)________________.</td><td>Examples
Would you like to play tennis?
How about playing tennis?
Let's play tennis.</td></tr>
<tr><td>Accepting
That sounds great.
I'd love to.
What a good idea.
That sounds like a lot of fun.</td><td>Declining
I'd love to, but I have to study for a test.
Thanks for asking, but I already have plans.
I'm afraid I can't.
Maybe some other time.</td></tr>
</table>

In each role play, one student will be Student A and the other student will be Student B.

1. Student A wants to go out for coffee with Student B after class. Student B declines because he/she has to work.
2. Student A wants to invite Student B to a dinner party at Student A's house this coming Saturday. Student B accepts the invitation. Students A and B discuss a time.
3. Student A wants to go to the movies with Student B on Friday night. Student B declines because he/she is going away for the weekend.
4. Student A wants to go shopping with Student B tomorrow afternoon. Student B is busy tomorrow afternoon but suggests going the day after tomorrow. Student A accepts. Students A and B decide on a place and time to meet.
5. Student A invites Student B to go camping for the weekend. Student B hates camping but doesn't want to hurt Student A's feelings. Because of this, B makes up an excuse and declines the invitation.
6. Student A invites Student B to play tennis. Student B is very tired and doesn't want to. Student A **keeps on** persuading Student B to play tennis. Student B finally accepts the invitation.

Now, work with your partner to create a dialogue for a scenario that you have recently been in that requires an invitation. After you have practiced, you may be asked to act the first part out in front of the class. Before Student B accepts or declines the invitation, ask the other students to guess what Student B will say. After they have guessed, continue acting it out. Did the other students guess correctly?

Small Talk

When people get together at school, at work, or in the neighborhood, they usually engage in "small talk." Small talk has been defined as "casual or trivial conversation." Small talk may not seem important, but it is a valuable social skill. Strangers also engage in small talk in places like the elevator, the doctor's office, or the airport. Whether you have met the person you are talking to before or not, small talk is very useful. Small talk usually involves talking about "safe" topics that are unlikely to offend anyone. These topics vary from country to country.

Where does small talk take place?

______________________ ______________________
______________________ ______________________
______________________ ______________________

Here are some safe small talk topics. Add a few more to the list.

movies ______________ ______________
the weather ______________ ______________

What are considered safe topics in your country?

______________________ ______________________
______________________ ______________________
______________________ ______________________

In America, some topics are considered to be more likely to offend people and, as a result, are usually avoided. Can you think of others?

How much someone makes ______________________
How much something costs ______________________
Politics ______________________
Religion ______________________
How old someone is ______________________

What are some inappropriate topics in your country?

______________________ ______________________
______________________ ______________________
______________________ ______________________

Talking with Strangers

Decide if the following scenarios fit into the small talk category or not based on if they are safe or not.

		Appropriate	Inappropriate
1.	Talking about a human interest story in the newspaper	________	________
2.	Criticizing all of the new movies	________	________
3.	Asking if someone got fired	________	________
4.	Asking someone if his/her marriage is breaking up	________	________
5.	Talking about summer plans	________	________

Role plays with strangers:

Working with a partner, finish the dialogues below.

1. You are in the waiting room at the doctor's office. A stranger starts talking to you.
   Stranger: It's a nice day, isn't it?
   You: ____
2. You are at the bus stop, and it is really cold outside. You've been waiting a long time for the bus. You start talking to the stranger standing next to you.
   You: ____
   Stranger: It sure is.
3. You are at the supermarket and notice the price of vegetables is very high this week. A stranger turns and starts talking to you.
   Stranger: ____
   You: I know! It wasn't this expensive last week.
4. Your turn. Describe a small-talk situation. Then write a dialogue to go with it.
   Stranger: ____
   You: ____

Having a Good Party

The following sentences are a list of things a good host or hostess should do when giving a party. But the sentences are not in the correct order. Write the numbers 1 through 6 in the answer blanks to show which item should be done first, which should be done second, and so on.

a. ________ Escort people to the door when they leave.
b. ________ Introduce people to each other.
c. ________ Greet your guests at the door.
d. ________ Say, "Thanks so much for coming."
e. ________ Take your guests' coats and hang them up.
f. ________ Make sure everyone has a good time.

Work with a partner and fill out the chart below.

You are a guest at a party. Think about some things you should and shouldn't do.

	Should do	Shouldn't do
before the party	plan ahead	________
during the party	________	________
after the party	________	________

Work with a partner and answer the questions.

1. How often do you have parties?
2. How often do you go to parties?
3. When was the last time you went to a party? What was the occasion?
4. Which do you prefer, big parties or small parties? Why?
5. What are some reasons people have parties?

   ________, ________, ________, ________,

   ________, ________, ________, ________.
6. What was one of the best parties you've ever been to? Why was it so great?

   ____

7. When you have a party, how do you invite people (phone, written invitation, etc.)? ______________________________
8. Is it common for people to send invitations in your country? For what occasions? ______________________________
9. How important are the clothes you wear to a party? Explain. ______________________________

____
10. Do you have any parties coming up in the near future? What are the occasions? ______________________________

It's Party Time

Working alone, look at the invitations here and on page 36. Based on what you see, decide who would send the invitations and for what occasion. After you have determined that, imagine that you are that person and fill out the invitations. Also, decide on the time, place, date, and any other information you think is necessary. When you are finished, show your invitations to your partner. Keep in mind that the images say a lot about the people sending the invitation and about the event itself.

HAPPY BIRTHDAY

Unit 5
Get Well Soon

You're in our prayers and thoughts.
Our love is with you.

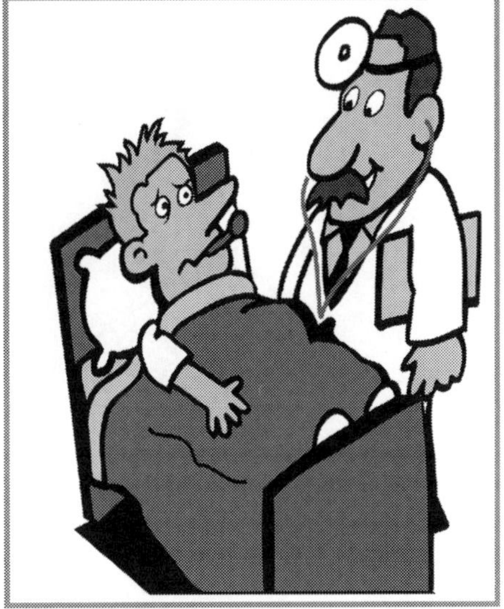

Hurry up and get better.
Doctor's orders.

Questions:

1. What is the difference between these two messages?
2. Who do you think would be given the first card?
3. Who do you think would be given the second card?
4. Paraphrase the two captions you just read. Paraphrasing means to restate something in your own words. Write them in the boxes below.

5. What are some words associated with hospitals and illnesses. List them below.

______________ ______________ ______________ ______________

______________ ______________ ______________ ______________

In the Hospital

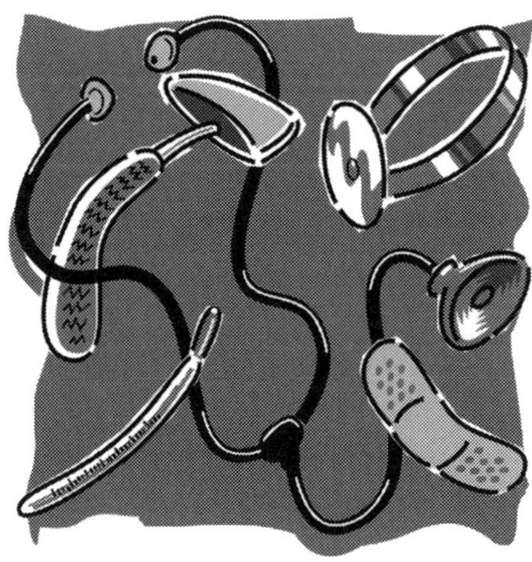

In a group, ask and answer the questions below.

1. Have you ever been in the hospital? If so, how long did you stay? __________
2. Many Americans don't enjoy the idea of going to the hospital. Give five reasons why you think this might be true.

   ____

   ____

   ____

   ____

   ____

3. How often do people in your country have **routine** physical exams? ________
4. How often do people in your country go to the dentist? ________________
5. What are some reasons people go to the hospital? List them below.

   ____________________ ____________________

   ____________________ ____________________

   ____________________ ____________________

6. Are nurses well respected in your country? What about doctors? __________

   ____

7. How often do you get sick? ______________________________
8. How often are you sick enough that you have to stay home in bed? ________

   ____

9. In your country, can people stay home from work when they are sick? If so, are they allowed a certain number of "sick days"? __________________

10. Do you think good health is created or inherited? ____________________
11. What do you usually do when someone you know is in the hospital? Do you visit? Send flowers? Send a card? ____________________
12. What do you do when you have a headache? (See the box below.)

When I have a headache, I ____________________ .
When I have a toothache, I ____________________ .
When I have a fever, I ____________________ .
When I have a stomachache, I ____________________ .
When I feel nauseous, I ____________________ .
When I have a sore throat, I ____________________ .
When I have a broken heart, I ____________________ .

Healthy Habits

With your group, discuss good and bad habits.

I think ____________________ is a good habit because ____________________ .
I think ____________________ is a bad habit because ____________________ .

Here are some examples.

"I think jogging is a good habit because it is good for the bones."
"I think eating too much fast food is a bad habit because it has a lot of fat."

Now think of three family members. First, write the person's name. Then write one healthy habit and one unhealthy habit about each person on the chart below.

Person	Unhealthy habit	Healthy habit
________	________	________
________	________	________
________	________	________

This is Bob. He is very nervous because he has a doctor's appointment tomorrow. He is not very healthy. He has bad eating habits. He almost always eats donuts for breakfast and fast food for lunch. He rarely eats fruits or vegetables, and he snacks all day long. He usually smokes a pack of cigarettes a day. He often drinks beer and whiskey at dinner. **On top of it all,** he never gets any exercise.

Bob wants to change **one thing at a time.** In what order should he change things?

1. First, he should ____ .
2. Then, he should ____ .
3. After that, he should ____________________________________ .
4. Next, he should ____ .
5. Finally, he should _______________________________________ .

What are Bob's bad habits?

-
-
-
-
-

What is your worst habit? Do you plan to change it? Have you already changed any bad habits?

Staying Healthy

Read the factors on the next page and circle how important you think each one is for a long, healthy, and happy life. After you have answered them on your own, discuss them with your classmates.

	very important				not important
1. Having a positive attitude	1	2	3	4	5
2. Helping others/volunteering	1	2	3	4	5
3. Taking a nap every day	1	2	3	4	5
4. Laughing a lot	1	2	3	4	5
5. Eating fish	1	2	3	4	5
6. Having a pet	1	2	3	4	5
7. Exercising regularly	1	2	3	4	5
8. Limiting alcohol	1	2	3	4	5
9. Getting enough sleep	1	2	3	4	5
10. Having good friends	1	2	3	4	5
11. Drinking water	1	2	3	4	5
12. Having regular checkups	1	2	3	4	5
13. Avoiding stress whenever possible	1	2	3	4	5
14. Limiting soft drinks	1	2	3	4	5
15. Taking vitamins every day	1	2	3	4	5
16. Avoiding late-night snacks	1	2	3	4	5
17. Quitting smoking	1	2	3	4	5
18. Being married	1	2	3	4	5

Add one more factor to this list. Star the five most important factors listed.

What Would You Do?

Look at the situations below. Read all of the possible answers and choose the best one. After that, work in a group and create one more answer for each scenario.

1. You have a low fever, a headache, and feel a little tired. You are supposed to go to work. What would you do?
   a. I would go to work even though I didn't feel very well.
   b. I would call in sick and rest for a few days.
   c. I would go to the clinic and see a doctor. I'll let the doctor decide if I should miss work or not.
   d. ____

2. You are in the hospital for a week because of minor surgery. Would you like to have visitors?
   a. Yes. I would want a lot of people to visit me.
   b. Yes, but only close friends and family.
   c. No. I would want everyone to stay away until I was feeling a little better.
   d. ______________________________
3. Your doctor says you should quit smoking and lose a few pounds. What would you do?
   a. I would go on a diet and quit smoking the next day.
   b. I would think about it but probably do nothing.
   c. I would think to myself, "No way."
   d. ______________________________
4. One of your friends is in the hospital. What would you do?
   a. I would send flowers and a card.
   b. I would send a huge box of chocolates.
   c. I would call to see if my friend wanted a visitor or not.
   d. ______________________________

Create one more scenario on your own.

____

____

a. ______________________________
b. ______________________________
c. ______________________________
d. ______________________________

Show it to your classmates and see which answers they choose. Did they choose the same answer as you would have chosen?______________________

I Need Some Advice

Practice these dialogues with a partner. Create your own dialogue using the cues below.

Alice and Beth work out at the same health club.

Alice: Can I ask you for some advice?
Beth: Sure. What is it?

Alice: I want to lose a few pounds. Any suggestions?

Beth: If I were you, I would walk to work in the morning.

Alice: What a good idea! Thanks for the suggestion.

Mark and Paul are co-workers.

Mark: Would you mind if I asked you for some advice?

Paul: Not at all. What is it?

Mark: I want to quit smoking. What should I do?

Paul: Why don't you drink water whenever you want a cigarette?

Mark: Hmmmm. I've never thought of that. Thanks.

1. stop biting my nails

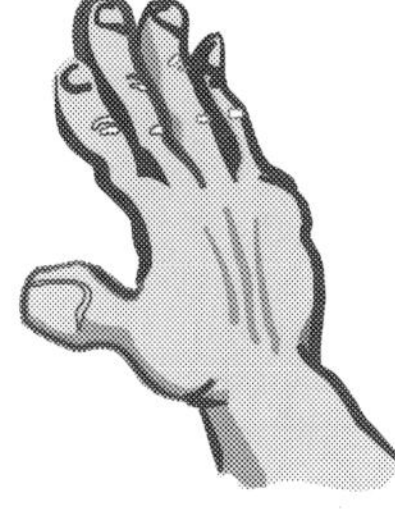

2. help a friend quit smoking

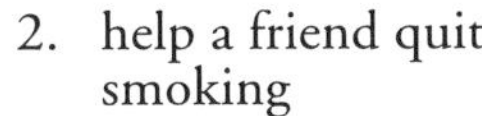

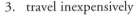

3. travel inexpensively

4. become a millionaire

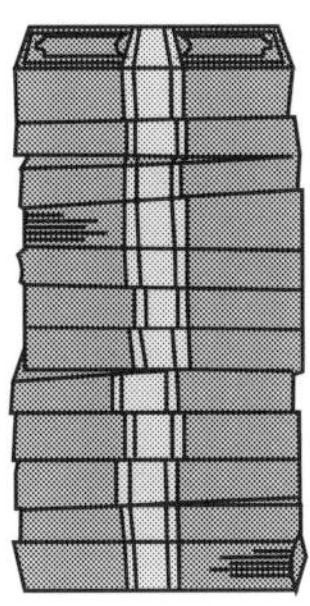

5. learn how to sing

6. Now it's your turn to come up with something!

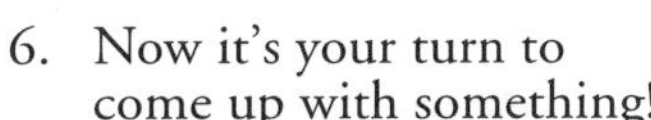

Create a Card

Go to a place that sells greeting cards and look at the get well cards. Choose three cards with very different messages. Sketch the image and write the caption of each card in the boxes below. If you prefer not to sketch, please write a description of the images instead.

Create a card for one of your co-workers:

One of your co-workers broke her leg in a skiing accident and has to spend a week in the hospital. She is recovering well, but you still want to send a card. Sketch or describe the image. Write a caption. Would it be OK to send her a humorous card, or should it be a serious one?

Unit 6
Happy Birthday to You!

Which of the three captions below would be the best caption for the image above? Why?

Have a moooo-velous birthday!
May all your dreams come true. Happy Birthday.
Have a nice birthday, but not during office hours. Happy Birthday!

Talking about Birthdays

Work in a group and discuss the questions below.

1. Do you enjoy celebrating your friends' birthdays? Why? ________________

   ____

2. Do you enjoy celebrating your own birthday? ________________
3. Which do you enjoy more, giving presents or getting them? Why? ________

   ____

4. How are birthdays celebrated in your own country? ________________

   ____

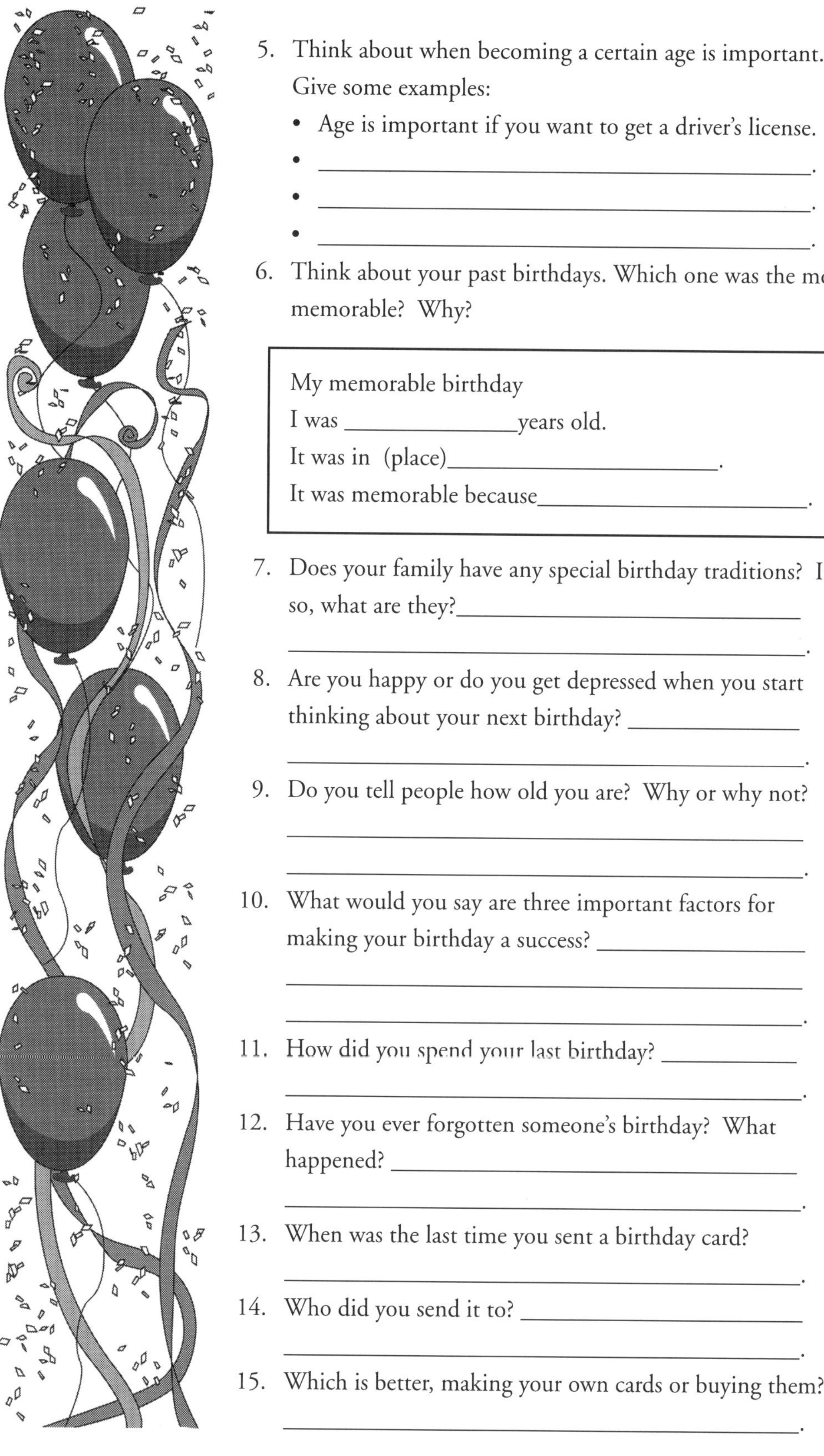

5. Think about when becoming a certain age is important. Give some examples:
   - Age is important if you want to get a driver's license.
   - ______________________________.
   - ______________________________.
   - ______________________________.
6. Think about your past birthdays. Which one was the most memorable? Why?

> My memorable birthday
> I was ____________ years old.
> It was in (place)____________________.
> It was memorable because____________________.

7. Does your family have any special birthday traditions? If so, what are they?______________________________
   ______________________________.
8. Are you happy or do you get depressed when you start thinking about your next birthday? ____________
   ______________________________.
9. Do you tell people how old you are? Why or why not?
   ____
   ______________________________.
10. What would you say are three important factors for making your birthday a success? ____________
    ____
    ______________________________.
11. How did you spend your last birthday? __________
    ______________________________.
12. Have you ever forgotten someone's birthday? What happened? ______________________
    ______________________________.
13. When was the last time you sent a birthday card?
    ______________________________.
14. Who did you send it to? ____________________
    ______________________________.
15. Which is better, making your own cards or buying them?
    ______________________________.

Make up your own questions about celebrating birthdays. Ask a partner your questions.

Complete the questions below.

How often do you ____?
When was the last time you _____________________________________?
Have you ever ____?

When you are finished, report one interesting birthday fact about your partner to the rest of the class.

An interesting fact about my partner: ______________________________

A Celebrity's Birthday Party

As a whole class, choose one celebrity to plan a party for. This person could be an actor, a writer, a musician, or a politician. After that has been decided, work in pairs to plan a birthday party for this famous person. You will have $500 to spend on this party. Follow the guidelines below. When you are finished, present your party plans to the rest of the class. The class will have a discussion and then vote to decide which party plans should be chosen.

Should it be a surprise? ______yes ______no

Where will it be held? Indoors or outdoors? Complete the lists and add more places where the party could be held.

Indoors		*Outdoors*	
restaurant	__________	backyard	________
home	__________	rooftop	________
office	__________	beach	________
cafe	__________	park	________

When will it be held? Circle one from each category.

Month: January, February, March, April, May, June, July, August, September, October, November, December
Day: Sunday, Monday, Tuesday, Wednesday, Thursday, Friday, Saturday
Time: Morning, afternoon, evening, night

Make a guest list. Write down the names of three other celebrities and why they are going to be invited.

1. ______________________________
2. ______________________________
3. ______________________________

What kind of food are you going to have? ______________________________
____

What activities are you going to plan for the party?

1. ______________ 4. ______________
2. ______________ 5. ______________
3. ______________ 6. ______________

Imagine the party budget has been reduced to $100. What changes would you have to make from above? ______________________________

Now that you are done, present these plans to your classmates. When every group has finished presenting, choose the group that has planned the best party.

Group:______________
Why these party plans are the best: ______________________________

An Invitation

No party is complete without an invitation. Using the information on the previous page, write out an invitation for the celebrity's party. If you have any party invitations at home, bring them to class and show them to your classmates.

Complete the invitation.
Put the information in any order you want.

date:

where:

why:

time:

My Own Birthday Celebration

You just spent time planning a party for a famous person.

What kind of party would you like to have for yourself?
How would it be different from the one you planned for the celebrity?

It's my birthday.
Imagine it were your birthday tomorrow and you could do anything you wanted.
How would you spend the day?
In the morning, I would ______________________________.
In the afternoon, I would______________________________.
In the evening, I would ______________________________.
After that, I would ______________________________.

Birthday Scenarios

Look at the situations below. Read all of the possible answers and choose the best one. After that, work in a group and create one more answer for each scenario.

1. Your birthday is **coming up** very soon. What would you do?
   a. I would start telling everyone now. I want them to plan a party for me.
   b. I wouldn't tell anyone. I don't like the fact that I'm getting older.
   c. I would tell everyone the day after my birthday.
   d. ______________________________
2. You have to buy a birthday present for your friend, but you don't have any extra money this month. What would you do?
   a. I would send a card.
   b. I would tell my friend that I am going to get a present next month.
   c. I would give my friend a coupon for one free housecleaning.
   d. ______________________________
3. Your friend gives you a present that you don't like **at all.** What do you say when you open it?
   a. "This is the most beautiful present I've ever received."
   b. "Thank you."
   c. "This is really ugly. Why did you bother?"
   d. ______________________________
4. You mention to your friend that you are planning a party for him. He says that he does not want anyone to celebrate his birthday. What would you do in this situation?
   a. I would still plan a party. Everyone likes parties.
   b. I would ask him again to see if he really meant what he said.
   c. I would forget the party and invite him out for a quiet dinner.
   d. ______________________________

Think about what you've learned in this unit.

What are three things that you've learned about your classmates?

I never knew that ______________________________ .

It was interesting to learn that ______________________________ .

I was surprised to hear that ______________________________ .

What Would Happen If . . .

Work in pairs or small groups and discuss the following.

What would happen if . . .

you forgot your friend's birthday?

someone you didn't know very well gave you a very expensive birthday present?

your friends had a surprise party for you?

someone you didn't know asked you how old you were?

someone asked an older person in your country how old he or she was?

you received a bouquet of birthday flowers from a secret admirer?

you couldn't blow out all of the candles on your birthday cake?

After discussing these situations, choose one and act it out in front of the class.

Birthday Cards

Look at these images. Then read each situation. Choose a card and write the appropriate caption. Keep the relationship and the age of the person you are giving the card to in mind when you are writing the caption.

Situation 1: You want to send a card to your five-year-old cousin	Situation 2: You want to send a birthday greeting to your friend living overseas.	Situation 3: You want to wish your boss (who has a very good sense of humor) a happy birthday.
cousin	friend	boss

Next to each person listed, write who should get which card. In the boxes below, write a caption for each card.

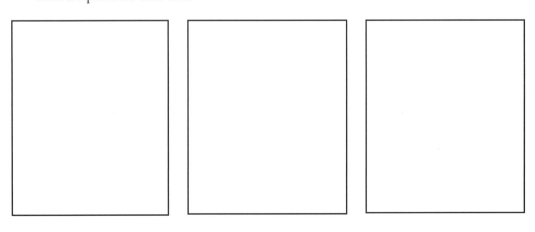

Unit 7
They're Getting Married

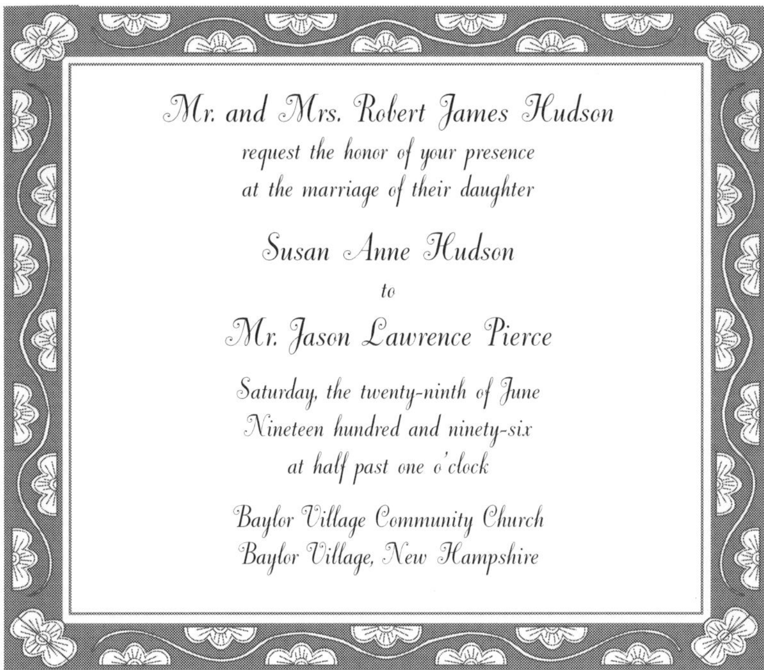

Mr. and Mrs. Robert James Hudson
request the honor of your presence
at the marriage of their daughter

Susan Anne Hudson
to
Mr. Jason Lawrence Pierce

Saturday, the twenty-ninth of June
Nineteen hundred and ninety-six
at half past one o'clock

Baylor Village Community Church
Baylor Village, New Hampshire

1. What is the bride's name?
2. What is the groom's name?
3. Who has sent the invitation?
4. When will the wedding take place?
5. Where will the wedding take place?
6. What is the date of the wedding?
7. When will the couple's anniversary be?
8. How would you describe the invitation? Is it formal or informal?
9. Do you think you would have to RSVP?
10. Have you ever received a wedding invitation like this?

Wedding Talk

In groups, answer the questions below.

1. How many weddings have you been to? ____________________
2. Which one was the most memorable? Why? ____________________

   ____

3. At what age do people in your country usually get married? ____________________
4. Describe a wedding ceremony in your country. ____________________

   ____

5. In your opinion, what is the best season for a wedding? ____________________
6. Why do you think so many people in America get married in June? Is there one month in your country that is more popular for weddings? ____________________

   ____

7. Do people in your country go on **honeymoons?** ____________________
8. If so, what destination is popular? ____________________
9. What does the idiom "to tie the knot" mean? Use it in a sentence. ____________________

   ____

10. What are some advantages and disadvantages of the following types of honeymoon trips?

	Advantages	Disadvantages
trip to a ski resort		
Caribbean cruise		
Tanzanian animal safari		

11. "Marriage is like a river; it's easier to fall in than out."

—Anonymous

Do you know what this quote means? Discuss it with your classmates. Do you agree or disagree? Why?

He's Going to Pop the Question

Tom is ready to ask Thelma to marry him. Yes, he's going to **"pop the question."** He has the ring and believes he is ready to **settle down.** He has one problem. He doesn't know where he should pop the question. He wants this to be a moment to remember. Can you help him?

Thelma
25 years old
Hobbies: reading, the symphony, jogging, and painting

Tom
27 years old
Hobbies: snorkeling, music, reading, and traveling

Should he pop the question . . .

1. on a cruise?
2. on the beach at sunset?
3. at an expensive French restaurant?
4. at a rock concert?
5. at the symphony?
6. at a basketball game?
7. at home in the living room?
8. ____________________
9. ____________________

10. Which of these places do you think would be the best and worst for him to pop the question? Why?
    best ______________________________
    worst ______________________________
11. Thelma wants very much to marry Tom. Do you think she should pop the question instead? ______________________________
12. Do women in your country ever ask men to marry them? ______________

Wedding Scenarios

Look at the situations below. Read all of the possible answers and choose the one you like best. After that, work in a group and create one more answer for each scenario. Finally, write your own scenario and give three possible solutions. Have a partner answer it.

1. Your best friend just became engaged to someone you don't like. What would you say when your friend tells you about the engagement?
    a. "I wouldn't marry him/her if I were you."
    b. "Oh, that's nice."
    c. "That's great. I'm so happy for you."
    d. ______________________________
2. You want a small wedding, and your fiancé(e) wants a large one. What would you do?
    a. I would talk to my fiancé(e), and we would hopefully compromise on a midsized wedding.
    b. I would do what my fiancé(e) wanted and would have a big wedding.
    c. I would keep on pushing until my fiancé(e) agreed to have a small wedding.
    d. ______________________________
3. Your wedding ring fell down the kitchen sink drain. What would you do?
    a. I would tell my spouse what happened.
    b. I would secretly go to the jewelry store and replace it.
    c. I wouldn't do anything. I would see how long it takes for my spouse to notice.
    d. ______________________________

4. You are happily married, but most of your friends are divorced. What would you do if your friends asked about your marriage?
   a. I would tell them how wonderful it was.
   b. I would briefly say that things were fine and then I'd change the subject.
   c. I would talk about the negative aspects of my relationship.
   d. ______________________________

5. ______________________________?
   a. ______________________________
   b. ______________________________
   c. ______________________________
   d. ______________________________

Dream Wedding

Work with a partner to create what you think would be the perfect wedding.

Who is getting married? (You may choose yourself, someone you both know, or even a historical figure.) ______________________________

What will the bride wear? ______________________________

What will the groom wear? ______________________________

Where in the world will the wedding take place? ______________________________

Is the wedding going to be traditional or original? ______________________________

Where will the bride and groom go on their honeymoon? ______________________________

What kind of reception will the bride and groom have? ______________________________

How many people will attend the wedding? ______________________________

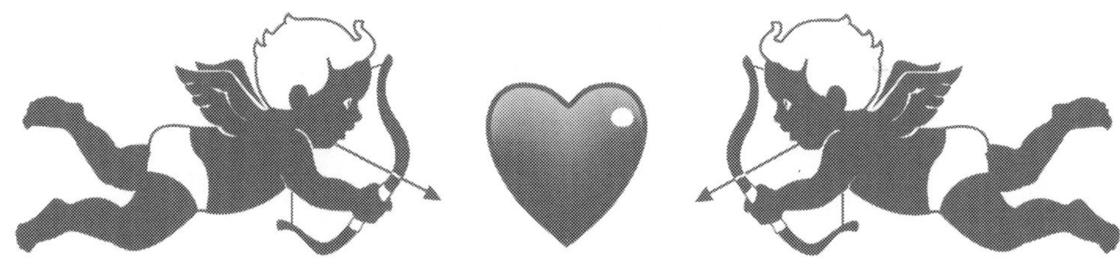

Until Death Do Us Part

Below are traditional Christian wedding vows said at many marriage ceremonies. "In the Name of God, I ____________, take you, ____________, to be my husband/wife, to have and to hold from this day forward, for better, for worse, for richer, for poorer, in sickness and in health, to love and cherish, until we are parted by death. This is my solemn vow."

1. Would you want vows like these read at your wedding? ________________
2. Do you agree or disagree with the message? ________________________
3. How would you paraphrase these vows? ___________________________

   ____

Here are ten factors generally considered to be important for a successful marriage. Rank them according to their importance to you.

1. patience	1. ____________________
2. kindness	2. ____________________
3. respect	3. ____________________
4. fair play	4. ____________________
5. honesty	5. ____________________
6. forgiveness	6. ____________________
7. laughter	7. ____________________
8. order	8. ____________________
9. remembrance	9. ____________________
10. love	10. ____________________

Are there any factors not listed that you would like to add? If so, please add them below.

________________ ________________ ________________

In pairs or small groups, use the cues below and discuss the factors listed above. Report back to the whole class when you've finished.

Patience is important because ______________________________________ .
I think laughter is important because__________________________________ .

A relationship needs to have ________________ because ________________ .
If a couple doesn't have ________________ then ______________________ .

Happy Anniversary

Once a couple is married, it is customary to give them an anniversary card each year on the anniversary of their marriage, especially if the people giving the card are the couple's family or good friends. Some spouses exchange cards on their anniversary. Others renew their vows on this day. There is a stereotype in America that husbands usually forget their anniversary. Is this true in your country?

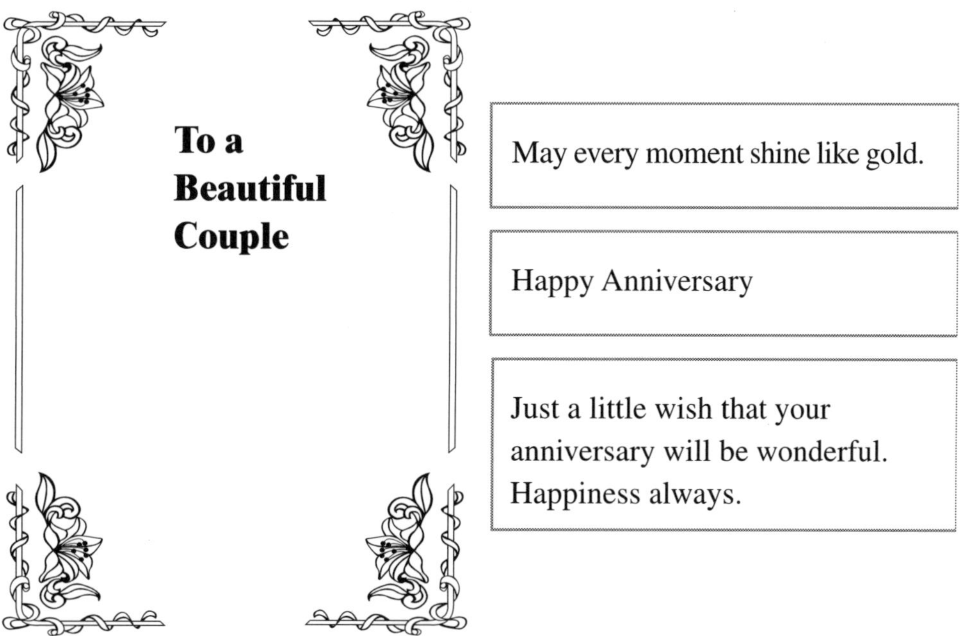

To a Beautiful Couple
May every moment shine like gold.
Happy Anniversary
Just a little wish that your anniversary will be wonderful. Happiness always.

1. Which caption do you like better?
2. Write one more caption for the anniversary card above.

caption:

A ring is given
A present is carried
but a good loud snore
means you're married.
Happy Anniversary.

Look at the caption above. What image would go well with it? You can either write about it or sketch it in the box below. Who do you think is giving the card? In what situations is this kind of humor appropriate?

Unit 8
You're Moving?

Life just won't be the same without you around. Don't forget us.

Home Sweet Home
Wishing you much happiness in your new home.

1. Why would someone send the card on the left?
2. Why would someone send the card on the right?
3. Have you ever received any cards like these?
4. Is moving something you look forward to? Why or why not?
5. What vocabulary would you expect to use if you were talking about moving?

Write some words in the spaces provided below.

________________ ________________ ________________

________________ ________________ ________________

Your House Is Beautiful

Once you have moved into your new home, you might want others to come and see it. If this is the case, you would invite them over for a housewarming party. This is usually a small party, and your friends come with housewarming gifts. This is a great chance for your friends to see your new place and for everyone to have an excuse to get together to have fun.

Some popular housewarming gifts are

- a plant
- a hanging board to hold keys
- a monogrammed doormat
- a bottle of wine or champagne

What kind of housewarming gifts would you like to receive?

______________	______________	______________	______________
______________	______________	______________	______________

Act out the following dialogue. Student A is a salesclerk in the home-furnishing department. Student B is looking for a housewarming gift for a friend.

A: May I help you?
B: Yes, I'm looking for a housewarming present. Any suggestions?
A: What about this small, blue rug?
B: It's beautiful, but it's too expensive.
A: How about his black reading lamp?
B: It's very nice, and the price is right. I'll take it.

Create your own dialogue using the pictures below or any other items you wish. You could look through a magazine and cut items out that you could give as a present and then use these items when acting out your dialogue.

Let's Talk about Moving

Work in small groups and answer the questions below.

1. How many times have you moved? ______________________
2. Think about all the places you have lived. Which place was your favorite? Why? ______________________
3. Do you think people enjoy moving? ______________________
4. Which do you prefer, renting a place to live or buying one? __________
5. What are the advantages and disadvantages of living in many different cities and/or countries? ______________________

Think about moving every year or two.	
Advantages	Disadvantages

6. What are the advantages and disadvantages of living in the same neighborhood throughout one's life? ______________________

Think about staying in the same neighborhood for a long period of time.	
Advantages	Disadvantages

7. Do people have housewarming parties in your country? If not, are there any other customs related to people moving into a new house? __________

____

8. At what age do children typically move out of the house and live on their own? ______________________________
9. Do you think families have to live close together in order to be a close-knit family? Why or why not? ______________________________

____

10. Do you prefer to live alone or with a roommate? Why? ______________________________

____

Can you think of any additional questions that you might like to ask your classmates about moving? Try using the sentence cues below.

Do people in your country ______________________________ ?
Have you ever ______________________________ ?
Do you think that you will ever ______________________________ ?

Moving Around

Look at the situations below. Read all of the possible answers and choose the best answer. Then work in a group and create one more answer for each scenario.

1. You're looking to buy a new house. A realtor calls and tells you there is a house for sale. The price seems too low. What would be the first thing you ask the realtor?
   a. "Is it in a safe neighborhood?"
   b. "How old is the house?"
   c. "Why is it so cheap?"
   d. ______________________________
2. Meeting your new neighbor, you say, "**Feel free** to come over anytime." Now your neighbor comes over every day. You are getting irritated with the situation. What would you do?
   a. I wouldn't answer the door.
   b. I would act rude. Hopefully, this would scare my neighbor away.
   c. Whenever my neighbor came over, I would say, "I'm busy. Sorry."
   d. ______________________________

3. Someone you don't know very well asks how much rent you pay. What would you say or do?
   a. I would tell. It really doesn't matter to me.
   b. "A reasonable amount for this area."
   c. "It's none of your business."
   d. ______________________________
4. A good friend is moving far away. What would you do?
   a. I would plan a farewell party.
   b. I would invite my friend over for a nice party.
   c. I don't like good-byes, so I wouldn't do anything.
   d. ______________________________

Using the cues below, discuss the four situations described above in more detail.

If I were in that situation, I would ______________________________ .
That actually happened to you? What did you do?
I would have done the same thing.
I don't think I would have done that. I would have ____________________ .

Teresa's Dilemma

Because of her job, Teresa will be moving to Los Angeles at the end of the month. Half of her is excited about the change, but the other half isn't. All of Teresa's friends are in New York, her family lives in a suburb outside of New York, and she doesn't know much about Los Angeles at all.

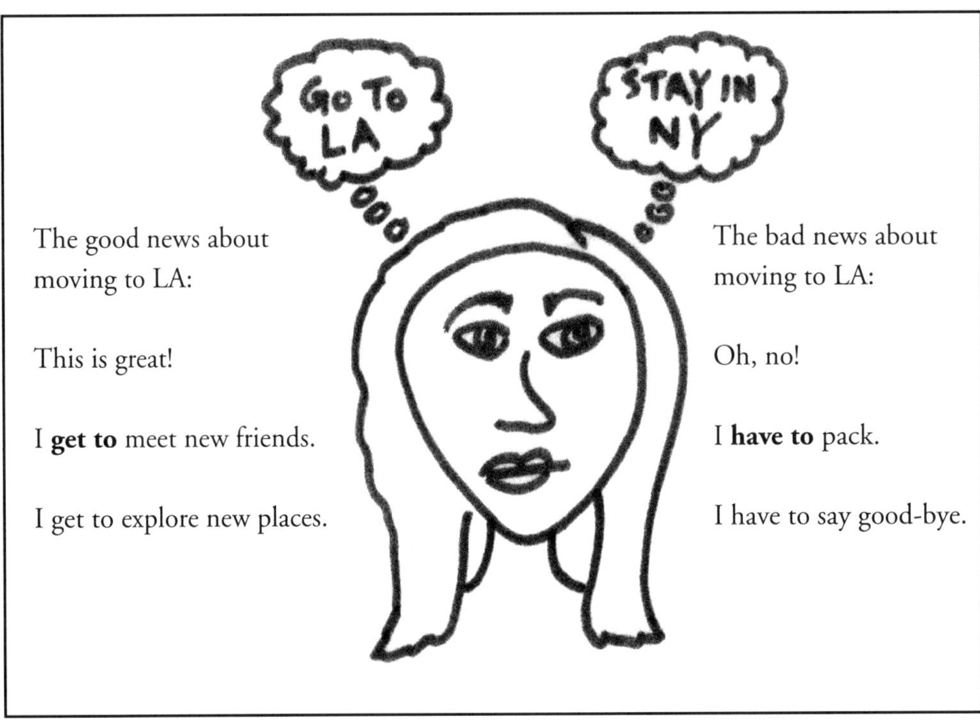

GO TO LA
STAY IN NY
The good news about moving to LA:
This is great!
I **get to** meet new friends.
I get to explore new places.
The bad news about moving to LA:
Oh, no!
I **have to** pack.
I have to say good-bye.

Imagine that you are moving to a new city next month. There are many things you have to do to prepare for the move. List them below.

I get to ____________________.　I have to ____________________ .
I get to ____________________.　I have to ____________________ .
I get to ____________________.　I have to ____________________ .
I get to ____________________.　I have to ____________________ .
I get to ____________________.　I have to ____________________ .

Talk to a partner about the things Teresa gets to do and the things she has to do.

She has to ______________________________ .
She gets to ______________________________ .

Design Your Dream House

After answering the questions below, design and sketch or describe in words your own dream house. Give a two-minute presentation of your ideas to the rest of the class. Many people have an idea about the house they would like to live in. For some, it would be a quiet log cabin in the mountains, and for others it would be a loft in New York City. Use the guidelines below to help you design your own house. Be creative and, because it is a dream house, don't worry about the cost.

Discuss the questions below.

1. Are your surroundings important to you? Why or why not? ______________

   ____
2. What is your favorite room in your house? ______________
3. Why is this your favorite room? ______________
4. Do you like where you live? ______________
5. If you could change anything about your home, what would it be?______________

   ____

Answer the following questions about your dream house.

Where would your house be? In the city, in the country, near the mountains, near the ocean, ______________

How big would your house be? ______________

What kind of house would you like to live in? A mansion, a **condominium,** an apartment, a **townhouse,** a tent, a camper, a houseboat, a **bungalow,** ______

____

What would your house look like inside?______________

Draw or write about your dream house in the box on page 68. Sketch the **floor plan** or describe it in words, too.

My dream house . . . I want to live in a red tent near the mountains. There won't be any furniture. It would be near a big lake.

Who do you think wants to live in the red tent? Why?

Send a Card to a Friend

Two people you know are moving. One person is your best friend. You have known this person for many years. The other person is someone you work with but don't know very well.

Choose a going-away card for both of the people who are moving. Write a caption for each card in the boxes below the two images. While you are writing the caption, **keep in mind** the relationship you have with each person.

Unit 9
When Are You Retiring?

Choose the best caption for each image.

A. Finally . . . you're going to have time for the important things in life. Good wishes for a happy **retirement**.

B. Retirement wishes especially for you. May all your plans turn out beautifully. Fill everyday with sunshine.

C. Hope you sail into retirement with ease. Best wishes to you.

Retirement Activities

When people think of retirement, they think of people who are sixty-five years old. That used to be the mandatory retirement age, but now the laws have changed. People are living longer, healthier lives, so they are also working longer than they did before.

People say that it is very important to keep busy during retirement. When people retire, they have to **figure out** how they want to spend their time. When a person retires, he or she has a good opportunity to start a new hobby, to volunteer, or to develop a new skill.

List of activities		
gardening	sewing	watching videos
acting	painting	making crafts
writing	cooking	collecting stamps
lifting weights	wood carving	volunteering
swimming	camping	fishing
hiking	golfing	dancing
bowling	investing in mutual funds	traveling
getting fit	photographing	surfing the Web
______________	______________	______________
______________	______________	______________

Work with a partner.

1. Add six more activities to the list.
2. Choose four activities you think your partner would be interested in during retirement.

   ______________, ______________, ______________, ______________

   Your partner will do the same for you.
3. Share your answers with your partner. Were you right?
4. What four activities would you choose for yourself?

   ______________, ______________, ______________, ______________

Categories:

Categorize the activities above into different groups. Put at least three activities into each box.

Outside activities	Expensive activities	Peaceful activities	Dangerous activities

Longer Life, Shorter Life

Some people think that a healthy lifestyle allows them to live a long, healthy life. They give up junk food, alcohol, cigarettes, coffee, soft drinks, and meat. Doctors say that if people give up these things, they will live longer. Other people don't spend their time worrying about this. They enjoy life, and that may mean eating a steak dinner, drinking too many glasses of red wine, smoking a few cigarettes, sipping espresso, and indulging in cheesecake all within a few hours. It certainly isn't the healthiest lifestyle, but these pleasures bring joy to a lot of people.

Which lifestyle would you choose? Why? ______________________________

Are you concerned about living a long life? If so, what are you doing about that now? ______________________________

Do you lead a healthy lifestyle? If so, how? ______________________________

If not, do you think you might adopt a healthy lifestyle as you get older? ________

____

What are the advantages and disadvantages of each lifestyle mentioned above?

Healthy lifestyle	Indulgent lifestyle

1. "We grow too soon old and too late smart."

—Pennsylvania Dutch saying

Why would someone say this? ______________________________

2. Which of these characteristics do you think are important as we age? Rank them in order of importance. Add two more to the list before you start.

• stable life	1. ______
• physically active	2. ______
• relaxed personality	3. ______
• flexible	4. ______
• curious	5. ______
• religious/spiritual	6. ______
• ______	7. ______
• ______	8. ______

3. How many **senior citizens** do you know? Do most of them seem happy or unhappy? ______
4. Do you think people look forward to retiring? ______
5. At what age do people in your country retire? ______
6. What should people do to make the transition to retirement easier? ______
______
7. At what age do you think you would like to retire? ______
8. Are the elderly respected in your country? ______
9. What role do the elderly play in your home country's society? ______
______
10. Is it common for the elderly to go into a nursing home or live with family members when they can no longer function by themselves? ______
______

Talking about Retirement

Look at the situations below. Read all of the possible answers and choose the best one. Then work in a group and create one more answer for each scenario.

1. You are about to retire from the company for which you've been working the past twenty-five years. What do you hope will happen?
   a. I hope that my co-workers will plan a huge party for me.
   b. I hope there will be a small luncheon for me before I leave.
   c. I hope my co-workers don't plan anything. I don't enjoy parties very much.
   d. ______

2. You are fifty years old. Your company offers you a lot of money to take an early retirement. What would you do?
   a. I would be very happy and accept the offer.
   b. I would decline and stay at the company. I'm too young to retire.
   c. I would retire and try to find a new job.
   d. ____
3. People are talking about retirement. What is your opinion?
   a. I think it is something to look forward to.
   b. I think it is something to be depressed about.
   c. I think it is good if the person retiring has a plan.
   d. ____
4. Someone you know retired last year. This person misses going to work each day. What would you say?
   a. "Maybe you should find a part-time job."
   b. "Stop complaining. You get to sleep late."
   c. "How about volunteering at an elementary school?"
   d. ____

Acting it out: Choose one of the scenarios from above and act it out with a partner. After you have practiced with your partner, act it out in front of the class. Once you have done this, create your own "retirement scenario." Don't tell your classmates who the characters are when you start to act it out. Instead, have them guess!

Before and After

Many people believe that there has been a significant event in their life that changed them forever. Rather than focus on the year of the event, they focus on the event itself. For some it was a pleasant event like marriage or the birth of a child. For others, the event wasn't a joyous occasion, yet it still changed things. These events may include the death of a family member or divorce.

"Once I got married, my life completely changed."
"Ever since Aunt Sally died, things changed."

Because these events are so important, the year of a particular event loses its importance.

What are some joyous and not so joyous "before and after" life events?

Joyous events	Sad events
1.	1.
2.	2.
3.	3.
4.	4.
5.	5.
6.	6.
7.	7.
8.	8.
9.	9.
10.	10.

Think about an important event in your life that you don't mind talking about.

What is the event? ____________________

What was your life like before this happened? ____________________

How did your life change after this event? ____________________

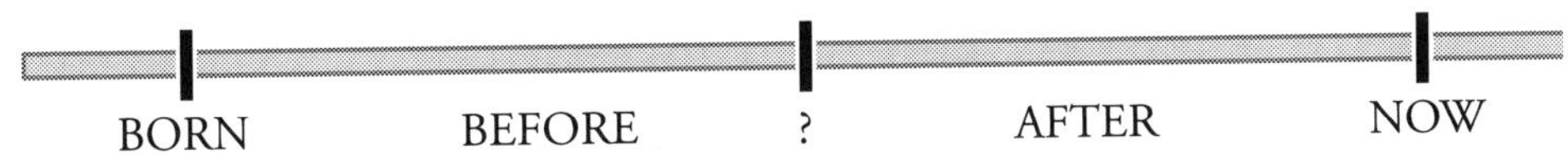

Time Lines

Make a time line of important events in your life. Use the words *first, then, after that, next, finally* when you write sentences about your life. Look at the examples on page 76.

First, I was born in Guatemala.
Then, my family moved to Argentina.
After that, I entered a technical college.
Next, I got married and had two children.
Finally, my family came to America.

Now, it is your turn.

First, ____.
Then, ____.
After that, ____.
Next, ____.
Finally, ____.

When you are finished, and only if you feel comfortable doing so, read your life experiences to your classmates.

"Aged," a Poem

Read the poem on page 77. In the boxes to the right, paraphrase each section of the poem.

1. What is the author's attitude about getting old? ____________________
   Give an example. ______________________________________
2. What images does the author give us about aging? ____________________
3. Choose four new words from the poem. Write them down in the first column of the list below.

New word	What I think it means	Dictionary definition
________	________	________
________	________	________
________	________	________
________	________	________

Discuss them with your classmates. After that, write what you think the meaning of each word is next to the word. Finally, ask your teacher to give you the definitions or use a dictionary and find them yourself. Were you right?

4. Do you agree with the author's view on aging? Why or why not? ___________

____

5. How do you view aging? ___________________________

Aged

The bountiful harvest of life.
Collected and gathered dreams.

Into a basket chock full of memories,
Recalled in delightful streams.

And laughter, oh, the laughter
Replace the work and toil

With the knee slaps and guffaws
Reaped from mineral rich soil.

This cultivated in the heart
Set forth the harvest's feast

Partake the succulent bowl of life
The spicy, the salty, the sweet

By
© DaNice Marshall

Talk About . . .

Work with a partner and discuss the things you have done in your life. Use the phrases in the box to help you form questions to ask your partner.

Talk about . . .	
places you have lived	parties you have planned
pets you have had	greeting cards you have received
pets you have wanted to have	strange things you have seen
people you have met	countries you have visited
people you have wanted to meet	people you have admired
sports you have played	overseas phone calls you have made
things you have lost	silly things you have done
things you have found	books you have read
hobbies you have had	movies you have seen
pleasant memories you have had	

Based on the interests of you and your partner, ask your partner questions. Look at the examples below.

Tell me about an interesting pet you or someone you know has had.
What is one of the silliest things you have ever done?
Tell me about a good book you have read.
Who is one person you have always wanted to meet?
How many parties have you planned?
What is one of the most interesting hobbies anyone you know has had?

Quotes:

1. "Age is like love, it cannot be hid." —Thomas Dekker

2. "We will be known forever by the tracks we leave." —Cherokee proverb

3. "Don't let yesterday use up too much of today." —Cherokee proverb

Discuss these statements with a partner. What do they mean? Are they true? Do you have any similar sayings in your language? Give a situation where someone would use these sayings.

When Are They Coming Back?

This is a picture of Fred and Nancy Hampton. Fred and Nancy just retired a few months ago, so they have been planning a month-long trip to France. They are very excited about their vacation. Their good friends have planned a **bon voyage** party for them. At this party, Fred and Nancy's friends will wish them a safe trip. In addition, their friends will give them a bon voyage card.

Look at the images below. Write a caption for each card. Which one would you give to Fred and Nancy?

Unit 10
Forever Friends

What kind of feelings do the two cards below evoke?

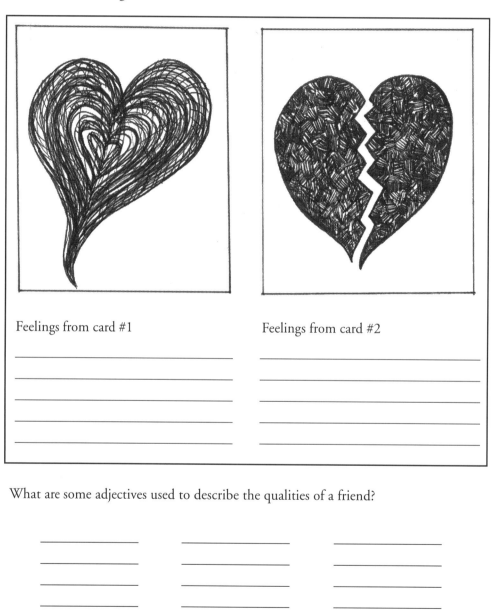

Feelings from card #1

Feelings from card #2

What are some adjectives used to describe the qualities of a friend?

Which three are the most important to you and your friendships?

______________ ______________ ______________

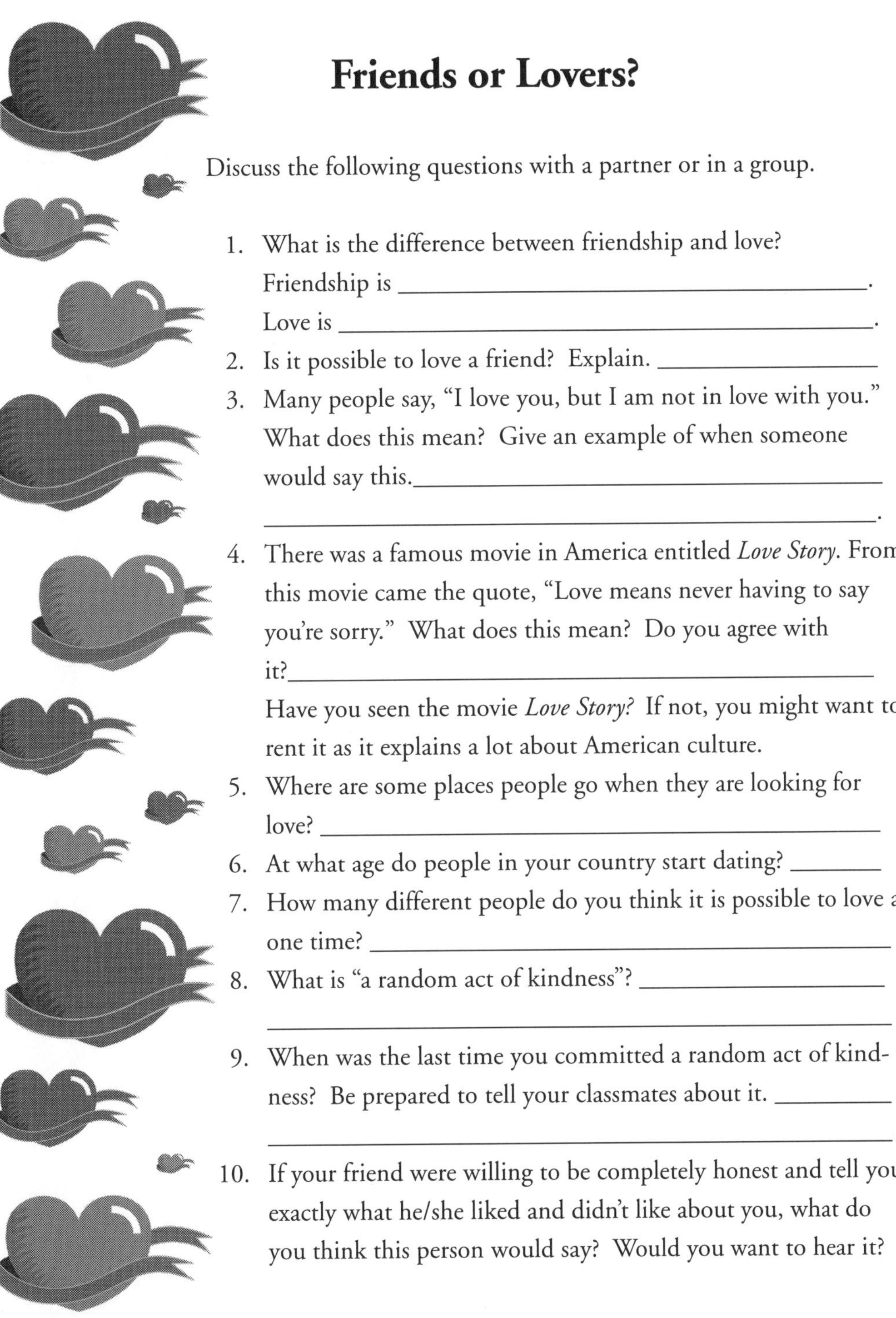

Friends or Lovers?

Discuss the following questions with a partner or in a group.

1. What is the difference between friendship and love?
   Friendship is ______________________________.
   Love is ______________________________.
2. Is it possible to love a friend? Explain. ______________
3. Many people say, "I love you, but I am not in love with you." What does this mean? Give an example of when someone would say this.______________________________
   ______________________________.
4. There was a famous movie in America entitled *Love Story*. From this movie came the quote, "Love means never having to say you're sorry." What does this mean? Do you agree with it?______________________________
   Have you seen the movie *Love Story?* If not, you might want to rent it as it explains a lot about American culture.
5. Where are some places people go when they are looking for love? ______________________________
6. At what age do people in your country start dating? ________
7. How many different people do you think it is possible to love at one time? ______________________________
8. What is "a random act of kindness"? ______________
   ____
9. When was the last time you committed a random act of kindness? Be prepared to tell your classmates about it. ________
   ____
10. If your friend were willing to be completely honest and tell you exactly what he/she liked and didn't like about you, what do you think this person would say? Would you want to hear it?

Positive things:

____________________, ____________________

____________________, ____________________

____________________, ____________________

Negative things:

____________________, ____________________

____________________, ____________________

____________________, ____________________

Quotes:

"One foe is too many and a hundred friends too few."

—Hopi proverb

"Friendship cannot be bought; you have to help make it."

—Cree proverb

" A friend in need is a friend indeed."

—English proverb

What do these proverbs mean?
Do you agree with them? Why or why not?
Do you have any proverbs similar to these in your language?

Friendly Dilemmas

Look at each situation below. Read all of the possible answers and choose the best one. Then, in a group create one more answer for each scenario.

1. You are at the movie theater waiting for a friend. You and your friend planned to meet at 7:00 P.M. Now, it's 7:30 P.M. and your friend still hasn't arrived. What would you do in this situation?
   a. I would go to a pay phone and try to call my friend.
   b. I would feel angry and leave.
   c. I would wait longer. Maybe something happened to my friend.
   d. ____

2. You find that you are falling in love with your friend. You've been friends since junior high school. What would you do?
   a. I would ignore the feelings. I wouldn't want to risk the friendship.
   b. I would send a card and sign it "from a secret admirer."
   c. I would be honest with my friend and say what I was feeling.
   d. ______________________________
3. You found out that one of your friends has just started dating your old boy/girlfriend. What would you do?
   a. I would be happy. Everyone deserves to have a love life.
   b. I would tell my friend to choose me or that other person.
   c. I would spend less time with my friend.
   d. ______________________________
4. You and your friend work at the same company. Your friend gets promoted and becomes your boss. What would you do?
   a. I would quit and get a new job.
   b. I wouldn't do anything. I'd be happy for my friend.
   c. I would ask to be transferred to a different department in the company.
   d. ______________________________

Get into pairs and create role plays using the situations above. When you are ready, act out one of the scenarios you have practiced in front of your classmates.

Remember: When "I would" is spoken, people usually use the contraction "I'd."

The Dinner Party

All of these people have been given magical powers to come alive for one evening. Work with a partner or in a small group and talk about the famous people and their autographs below. You might want to go to a library and look at an encyclopedia to find out more about them. Then decide who should be invited to the dinner party and where he or she should sit. You are not limited to the people on this list. You can choose anyone you want as long as your partner or group is in agreement. When you are finished working in groups, work as a class and come up with one final guest list.

Who on the list do you know?
What has made these people famous?

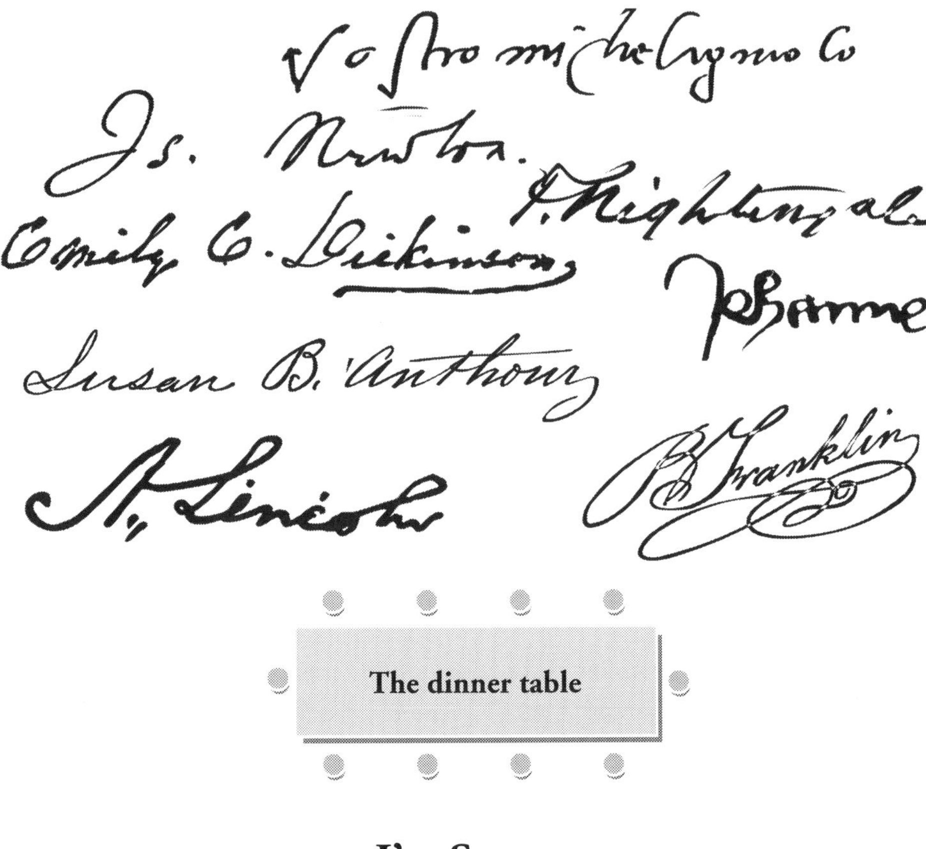

I'm Sorry

Sometimes we use the phrase "I'm sorry" to apologize, and sometimes we use it when we want to express sympathy. If you step on someone's foot, you might apologize and say, "I'm sorry." If your friend loses his job, you may feel bad about his or her situation. If this is the case, you would probably say, "I'm sorry" or "I'm sorry to hear that."

Talk about and answer the questions with a partner.

1. Give some situations when people would apologize and say, "I'm sorry."
   ____________, ____________, ____________
   ____________, ____________, ____________
2. When was the last time you used this expression? What were the circumstances? ____________
3. Who in your opinion spends more time apologizing, men or women? How did you come to this conclusion? ____________
   ____

4. Give two examples of when someone would use the expression, "I'm sorry to hear that." This is usually in response to bad news.
   A: ____________________
   B: I'm sorry to hear that.
   A: ____________________
   B: I'm sorry to hear that.
5. Do Americans apologize more or less than people in your country? ________
6. Look at the relationships below. Think of a possible reason why the person on the left would apologize to the person on the right. Write your answer in the space provided for you. Work in pairs or small groups.
   brother/sister ____________________
   sister/brother ____________________
   teacher/student ____________________
   student/teacher ____________________
   boyfriend/girlfriend ____________________
   girlfriend/boyfriend ____________________
   friend/friend ____________________
   teenager/parent ____________________
   parent/teenager ____________________
   salesclerk/customer ____________________
   person on the train/person on the train ____________________
   pilot/passenger ____________________
   secretary/boss ____________________
   boss/secretary ____________________
   driver/police officer ____________________
   waiter/guests ____________________
   defendant/judge ____________________
   wife/husband ____________________
   husband/wife ____________________
   pet owner/pet ____________________

Choose one of the situations above and act it out in front of the class. Let your classmates guess which situation you picked.

The Love Doctor Is In

Dear Dr. Love,

I think my boyfriend is cheating on me, but I am not sure. I don't know what to do. What would you do if you were in my situation?

—Losing Love In LA

Dear Dr. Love,

My best friend just got married, so now he doesn't have much time to spend with me. What should I do?

—Ditched in Dallas

Dear Dr. Love,

I want to ask my next door neighbor out on a date. I'm very nervous about this. What if I say or do the wrong thing?

—Tongue-Tied

Dear Dr. Love,

I am moving to a new city next month. I have a girlfriend, but she'll be staying here. Everyone tells me that long-distance relationships don't work. Should I end mine? Do you have any suggestions?

—Faraway Love

Dear Dr. Love,

I just moved to a new city, so I don't know that many people. I'd like to meet some new friends. What do you think I should do?

—Friend Seeker

Dear Dr. Love,

My best friend started a new job, so now there's no time for me. I'm so sad. Any ideas about what I should do?

—Job over Me

Dr. Love has received a lot of letters asking for advice this week. Help him out and give some advice to the people who wrote to him. When you are done, write your own letter to Dr. Love. Exchange letters with a partner and then answer the letter by giving some advice. Try using the phrases at the bottom of the page.

Asking for advice:
Do you have any suggestions?
What would you do if you were in my situation?
What do you think I should do?
Any ideas about what I should do?
Can you give me some advice?

Offering advice:
Why don't you ____________________?
If I were you, I would____________________.
Have you considered ____________________?
Maybe you should____________________.
I think you should____________________.
How about ____________________?

Celebrating Friendship, Celebrating Love

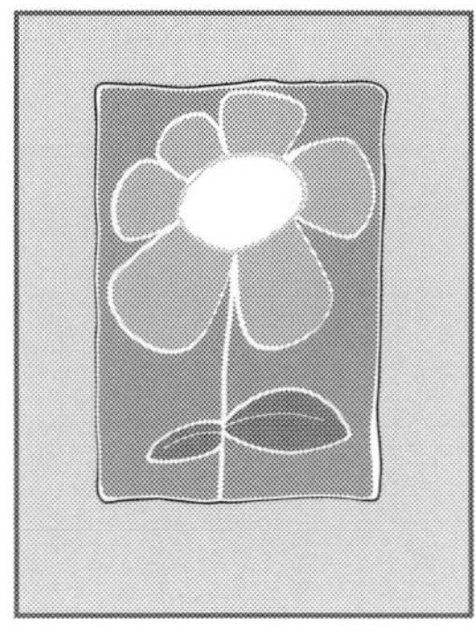

You feel grateful that you have such a good friend. Write a caption expressing this in the box below.

You want to profess your love to that special person you just met. Write a caption expressing this idea.

You want to confirm the love you have for that person you have been with for so long. Write a caption for this card.

Before writing the captions, spend a few minutes brainstorming. What vocabulary do you **associate** with each topic? Write down whatever comes to mind. When you start writing your caption, look at the list you came up with. It may give you some ideas.

Friendship	New love	Old love
____________	____________	____________
____________	____________	____________
____________	____________	____________
____________	____________	____________
____________	____________	____________
____________	____________	____________

Unit 11
With Deepest Sympathy

Read the captions. Which one do you like better, the shorter one or the longer one? Why?

With
deepest sympathy

In deepest sympathy
May you find comfort in
knowing that God has
prepared a glorious
place for your loved one.

1. What do you think the theme of this unit is going to be? How do you know?
2. Which card do you like better?

Over the Rainbow

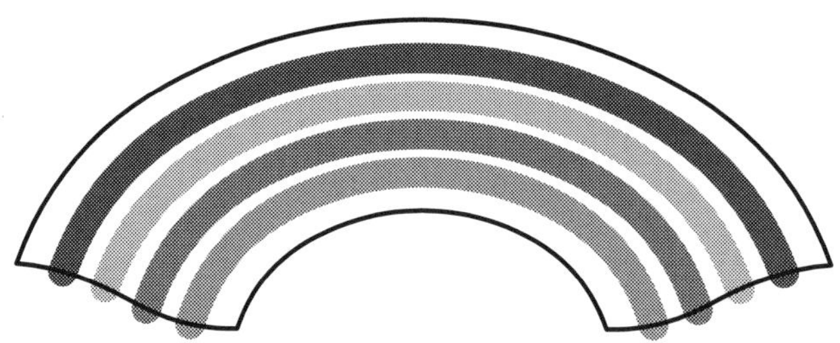

Rainbows (author unknown)

**Rainbows would never be rainbows,
If sunshine never met rain.
No one would ever need comfort,
if there were no sadness or pain.
But life holds both sunshine and flowers.
The days aren't all bright and fair,
so look through the showers for the rainbows.
You'll always find hope shining there.**

1. What kind of feeling does this poem express?
2. When would someone want to read a poem like this?
3. How many words in the poem rhyme?
4. What do rainbows symbolize for you?
5. Why do you think so many people enjoy looking at rainbows?
6. Optimists always see the positive side of things. Pessimists always focus on the negative. Optimists say, "the glass is half full" while pessimists say "the glass is half empty." One joke goes like this: "What's the difference between an optimist and a pessimist?" The answer is this: "An optimist invented the plane; a pessimist invented seat belts."

Would you consider yourself an optimist or a pessimist? ______________________
Give an example. ____

Sad Good-byes

Answer the questions below.

1. In America, death is very difficult to talk about. Is this true in your country? Why or why not? ___________________________
2. What are **funerals** like in your country? ___________________________
3. In America, people are expected to wear dark colors when attending a funeral. What is the custom in your country? ___________________________
4. Before the funeral service, people in America often attend a wake, which is basically a time before the burial when friends and relatives meet to remember the dead person. Do people in your country have a similar custom? ________
5. In America, people send flowers and **condolence** cards to the **grieving** family. What do people do in your country? ___________________________
6. Look at this proverb from a Native American tribe.
   "Life is not separate from death. It only looks that way."
   What is the main idea of this proverb?
   Rewrite the proverb in your own words. ___________________________

   ____
7. There is a religious group of people in America who call themselves Quakers. They have a very different custom regarding funerals. Read the following quote from someone who attended a Quaker funeral.

   "I attended the funeral service of my friend's grandmother. I was good friends with Maddy, a wonderful old woman who spent her life working at the local art museum. Her family was Quaker, so they followed Quaker customs when someone died. It was an extremely beautiful service. After Maddy passed away, one of her friends told everyone the bad news. That Sunday, everyone who wanted to attended the service and sat on a rug in a circle on the floor. There was a candle burning in the middle of the circle. People sitting in the circle spoke freely of their memories of Maddy. Nothing was rehearsed. All of the memories were loving. There was even a little laughter when people shared funny stories. When no one had anything else to say, the service was over. At the very end, people joined hands and prayed together. It was so simple, yet so elegant. That is one experience that I will never forget."

   —Paul, 45

- What do you think about this kind of **memorial service?**
- Do you think you would feel comfortable attending this kind of service?
- What is the purpose of having a memorial service or funeral?
- Do you think laughter is acceptable at this kind of event? Why or why not?

Unexpected News

Look at the situation below. Read all of the possible answers and choose the best one. After that, work in a group and create one more answer for each scenario.

1. Someone at work has died. You are expected to go to the funeral, but you don't deal with death very well. What would you do?
   a. I wouldn't go. There are going to be three hundred other people there, so I wouldn't be missed.
   b. I would go. I realize death is part of the life cycle.
   c. Instead of going, I would send a bouquet of flowers and a card expressing my sympathy.
   d. ______________________________
2. Your friend's dog was recently hit by a car and died. Your friend has been upset and tearful for the past week. What would you do?
   a. I would tell my friend to stop crying. It was only a dog.
   b. I would invite my friend to a concert to get his mind off his dog.
   c. I would offer to get my friend a new dog.
   d. ______________________________
3. A co-worker went home for the weekend to attend a funeral. What would you do when you saw this person on Monday?
   a. I would ask about the funeral.
   b. I would talk to this person, but I wouldn't mention the funeral.
   c. I would avoid my co-worker. Talking about death is too difficult.
   d. ______________________________
4. Working in pairs, write your own scenario but not any answers. Exchange papers with another pair of students. Each person writes two answers for the other group's scenario. When you are finished, exchange papers so you have your original scenario.

Then read your scenario and the one answer you like the best to the entire class.

scenario: ____
____

a. ____
b. ____
c. ____
d. ____

The Florist

In America, it is very popular to send flowers for a variety of reasons. It might be because your friend just gave birth to a beautiful baby, or a family friend has just retired after working forty years, or it might be because someone has **passed away.** No matter what the occasion is, there is always a perfect flower arrangement.

You want to order some flowers to be sent to a friend. You call the local florist to order them. After practicing the model dialogue, work with a partner and make up new dialogues using the information below.

A: Harland's Flower Shop, may I help you?
B: Yes, I'd like to order some flowers.
A: Okay. Who do you want to send them to?
B: Martha Bennett. M-A-R-T-H-A B-E-N-N-E-T-T.
A: What is the address?
B: 1378 Main Street.
A: Where is that?
B: Madison, Wisconsin.
A: What kind of flowers would you like?
B: I'd like an arrangement that costs $25 and includes some carnations.
A: That's no problem. Would you like to include a card?
B: Yes. Please say, "Good luck! Love, Bob."

A: When would you like the flowers delivered?

B: Tomorrow if possible.

A: Tomorrow it is. And how would you like to pay for it?

B: Put it on my MasterCard. My number is 5729-9889-8276.

A: What's your name?

B: Bob Driscoll.

A: Well, I have all of the information I need. Thanks for using Harland's Flower Shop.

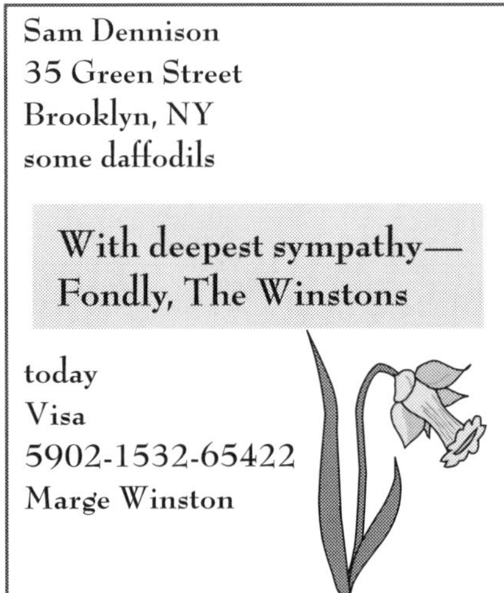
Sam Dennison
35 Green Street
Brooklyn, NY
some daffodils

With deepest sympathy—
Fondly, The Winstons

today
Visa
5902-1532-65422
Marge Winston

Patricia Miller
589 West 45th Street
New York, NY
a dozen long-stemmed roses

Please forgive me,
Love always, Steve

this afternoon
American Express
4922-0184-9229
Steve Boyd

A Sympathy Card

Someone you know has died. Choose an appropriate card and caption to send to the family. Keep in mind you don't know the family very well.

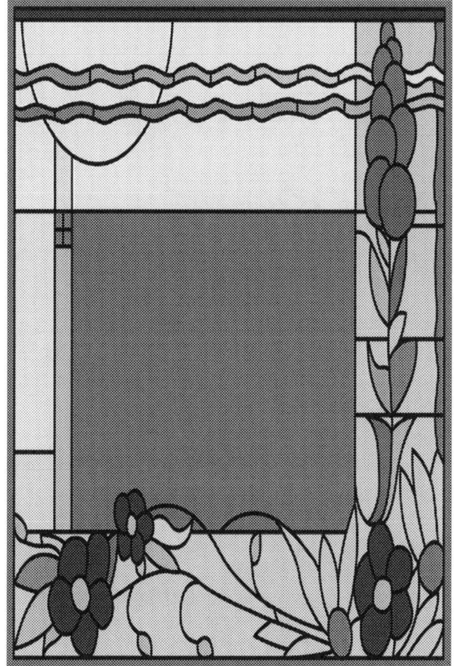

Love is all.
Love lives forever.
With deepest sympathy

In deepest sympathy
May you find contentment
in your heartfelt memories.

Which card is more appropriate? ______________________________

Which caption is more appropriate? ______________________________

Why do you think so? ______________________________

"When good men die, their goodness does not perish."

—Euripides

What does this quote mean? Do you agree with it? ______________________________

Unit 12

Thank You So Much

Look at the following cards. Read the captions below them and then write one more thank you caption for each of the cards.

Roses are red,
violets are blue
I am sending this card
to say "THANK YOU" to you.

The grass is green
and the sky is blue.
Without friends like you
What would we do?

Your caption:

Your caption:

Thank Who?

Work with a partner and discuss the questions below.

1. Name some situations that require someone to thank another person.

   ______________________ ______________________

   ______________________ ______________________

   ______________________ ______________________

2. How many times do you hear the words *thank you* each day? ____________
3. Have you ever sent a thank you card to someone? If so, what was the reason?

   ____

4. Has anyone ever forgotten to say "thank you" to you? If so, how did that make you feel? ______________________________________
5. How do people in your country typically express gratitude? ____________

   ____

6. When was the last time you said "thank you" to someone? What was the reason? ______________________________________
7. When was the last time someone said "thank you" to you? What was the reason? ______________________________________
8. List some occasions when a stranger would thank you. Then list some reasons when you would thank a stranger.

   Reasons why a stranger would thank me: Reasons why I would thank a stranger:

   ______________________ ______________________

   ______________________ ______________________

   ______________________ ______________________

9. In America, people sometimes leave a tip as a way of saying "thank you." A tip is a monetary gift usually given to those who have done some service. Some people who receive tips are waiters and waitresses, hairdressers, taxi drivers, delivery people, and **bellhops**. List some places and/or situations where leaving a tip would be expected.

   ______________ ______________ ______________

   ______________ ______________ ______________

   ______________ ______________ ______________

10. What is your opinion of tipping? Do people in your country tip? Explain any differences you have observed between the tipping customs in your country and those in America. ______________________________________

    ____

11. In America, tipping between 15 and 20% is customary in restaurants. Some people feel that if the service is really bad, they shouldn't leave a tip. Have you ever experienced bad service? If so, what happened? ____________________

____

12. Look at the Native American proverb below. Discuss it with a partner. After that, rewrite it in your own words. Do you agree with it? Why or why not?

"Where there is true hospitality, not many words are needed."

—Native American proverb

____

____

Your Turn

Look at the situations below. Read all of the possible answers and choose the best one. Then work in a group and create one more answer for each scenario.

1. You just had a very pleasant dinner at your co-worker's house on Saturday. What would you do the next day?
   a. I would sleep late and do nothing.
   b. I would send a thank you card.
   c. I would call and thank the person over the phone.
   d. ____
2. You lose your wallet at the shopping mall. One week later, someone calls to tell you that she found your wallet. She goes to your house to return it. When she returns it, you look and see that all of the money is still in it. What would you do after she gave it to you?
   a. I would thank her.
   b. I would give her a small cash reward.
   c. I would invite her to stay for coffee.
   d. ____
3. You are going to the post office, and a stranger holds the door open for you. How would you respond?
   a. I would say, "Thank you."
   b. I would just smile.
   c. I wouldn't do anything.
   d. ____

4. Your friend knows it is your birthday and gives you a present. When you open the box, you see an ugly sweater. What would you do?
   a. I would thank my friend for remembering my birthday.
   b. I would ask if I could exchange it for something else.
   c. I would put it on and happily wear it for the rest of the day.
   d. ____

Discuss the following questions.

1. Have you ever been in any situations similar to these?
2. What was the worst gift you ever received? What did you do?
3. Have you ever lost anything important? Was it returned to you?
4. When was the last time someone held the door open for you? Where were you? Did you respond? If so, what did you do?

I Want to Thank You

Work with a partner and practice the role plays below. One student will be Student A and the other will be Student B. Be prepared to act out one of the role plays you have practiced in front of the class.

Situation 1:

Student A is about to leave Student B's house. Student B cooked a great dinner and had an interesting group of friends over. Student A had a very good time and wants to thank Student B for everything.

Situation 2:

Student A is carrying a lot of packages and can't open the door to the apartment building. Student B is going into the apartment at the same time and holds the door open for Student A. Student A wants to thank Student B even though they don't know each other.

Situation 3:

Student A is at work but can't get the photocopier to work. Student B, a co-worker in the same department, helps Student A, and now the photocopier works. Student A wants to thank Student B for taking the time to help.

Situation 4:

It is Student A's birthday, and Student B, a friend, gives Student A a present. Student A opens the gift to find that it is a book he/she already has. Student A thanks Student B for the book. Will Student A be honest or not?

Situation 5:

Work with a partner and spend five minutes writing out a dialogue for a situation. Student A thanks Student B for something. Based on what the two of you say, your classmates have to guess the situation and why Student A is thanking Student B.

Situation 6:

Choose one of the situations above. Instead of being polite, Student A is going to act very rude and ungrateful. Have your classmates guess which situation you and your partner are acting out.

How To Do It

Thanking someone:	What are some other ways to say it?
Thanks for ________________.	____________________
Thanks a lot.	____________________
Thank you very much.	____________________

How To Do It

Responding to someone thanking you:	What are some other ways to say it?
You're welcome.	____________________
My pleasure.	____________________
I was happy to do it.	____________________

Create a Situation

Choose a person and a situation from the lists below or add your own. Based on your selection, write a short note thanking the person for whatever he or she did.

The person:	The situation:
a neighbor	This person you want to thank . . .
a good friend	taught you many things.
a family member	cheered you up.
someone at work	invited you for dinner.

a police officer	saved your life.
a boy/girlfriend	gave you beautiful flowers.
a husband/wife	typed your report.
a teacher	cared for your children.
______________	__________________
______________	__________________

THANK YOU
Thank You!
Thank You!

I can't thank you enough!
(add your personal message here)

____
____
____
____
____

Who Gets What Card?

Look at the cards below. Working in a small group, decide on an occasion and then write a caption for each card. These cards are not limited to one particular occasion. When you are done, report the captions your group wrote to the whole class. See what occasions other groups were thinking about for each card.

More Cards

Continue doing the same with these cards. Decide on an occasion and then write a caption for each card in the space provided. Compare the captions your group wrote with those of your classmates. Have fun!

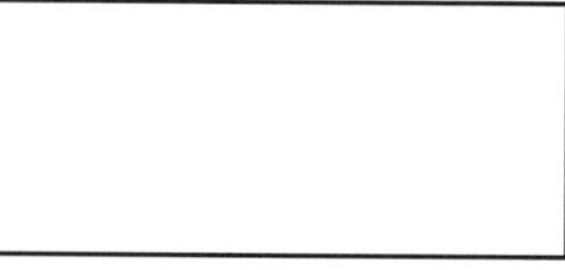

The End

In these units, you learned a lot about the special occasions in a person's life and the greeting cards that go with them. Your final assignment is to go to a place that sells greeting cards and take a look at the greeting cards. Choose three different cards and sketch or write a few sentences about the image on the card in the boxes on page 104. Write the caption under the image. You will give a short presentation to the rest of the class. In your presentation, include the following:

1. Explain the caption and the image of the cards.
2. Tell why you chose these three cards.
3. Talk about which of the cards you would rather send and which ones you would rather receive. Explain why.
4. Are cards like these available in your country?

When everyone has finished giving his or her presentation, discuss the following questions in small groups.

1. Did you enjoy looking for these three greeting cards? ____________________
2. Is it easier for you to read and select greeting cards now than it was before? __
____

3. What are some interesting things you have learned about American culture?
    - ______________________
    - ______________________
    - ______________________
4. What are some interesting things you have learned about your classmates' cultures?
    - ______________________
    - ______________________
    - ______________________
5. Which unit did you like the best? Why? ______________________
6. Which unit did you like the least? Why? ______________________
7. Do you think you will be sending more cards? ______________________
8. What special occasion is the most important to you now? ______________________

Glossary

Unit 1

page 2, all over = everywhere
page 3, fall into = to contain two or more groups
page 3, sentimental = based on or connected with feelings
page 6, anonymous = unknown by name
page 6, for now = used when something is happening now but might change in the future

Unit 2

page 10, a waste of time = not worth the time
page 13, sign = a description of your character and the things that will happen to you based on the position of the stars or planets at the time of your birth; a horoscope
page 13, spoiled = someone, especially a child, who is rude and gets whatever he or she wants
page 14, associated = to be connected with a particular subject, activity, etc.

Unit 3

page 20, psychics = a person having the ability to know what will happen in the future
page 21, superstitious = influenced by old-fashioned beliefs about luck and magic
page 21, keep quiet = to not say anything

Unit 4

page 29, RSVP = a French phrase used on invitations asking the person to tell the host or hostess whether or not he or she is going to the particular party or event in question
page 31, to keep on = to continue

Unit 5

page 38, routine = the normal and usual way in which you do things
page 40, on top of it all = in addition
page 40, one thing at a time = finish one task before starting another one

Unit 6

page 50, coming up = approaching
page 50, at all = used in questions and negative statements to emphasize what you are saying

Unit 7

page 54, honeymoon = a trip taken by two people who have just gotten married
page 55, pop the question = to ask for someone's hand in marriage
page 55, settle down = to start living in a place with the intention of staying there

Unit 8

page 64, feel free = used to tell someone you are happy if they do something
page 66, get to = to be able to do (has a positive meaning)
page 66, have to = something you must do
page 67, condominium = an apartment building where each unit is owned individually
page 67, townhouse = a house in a group of houses that share one or more walls
page 67, bungalow = a small cottage, usually one story
page 67, floor plan = a drawing or description of the shape of a room or area in a building and the position of the things in it
page 69, keep in mind = remember

Unit 9

page 70, retirement = when a person stops working at the end of his or her working life

page 70, figure out = to find an answer

page 73, senior citizen = an old person, especially someone who is over 60 years of age

page 79, bon voyage = a French phrase used to wish someone a good journey

Unit 10

page 85, defendant = the person in a court of law who has been accused of doing something illegal

page 88, associate = to make a connection in your mind between one thing or person and another

Unit 11

page 91, funeral = a religious ceremony held before burying or burning a dead person

page 91, condolence = sympathy for people who have had something bad happen to them, especially when someone has died

page 91, grieving = feeling extremely sad, especially when someone has died

page 92, memorial service = something done in order to remind people of someone who has died

page 93, passed away = a nice way to say that someone died

Unit 12

page 97, bellhop = a person employed by a hotel who assists guests by carrying luggage and running errands